ENVIRONMENT and COGNITION

ENVIRONMENT and COGNITION

edited by
WILLIAM H. ITTELSON
ENVIRONMENTAL PSYCHOLOGY PROGRAM AND
CENTER FOR RESEARCH IN COGNITION AND AFFECT
GRADUATE CENTER
CITY UNIVERSITY OF NEW YORK
NEW YORK, NEW YORK

1973
SEMINAR PRESS New York London
A Subsidiary of Harcourt Brace Jovanovich, Publishers

SEMINAR PRESS, INC.
111 Fifth Avenue, New York, New York 10003

United Kingdom Edition published by
SEMINAR PRESS LIMITED
24/28 Oval Road, London NW1

LIBRARY OF CONGRESS CATALOG CARD NUMBER: 72-7698

PRINTED IN THE UNITED STATES OF AMERICA

Contents

CHAPTER III

CHAPTER IV

CHAPTER V

CHAPTER VI

List of Contributors

Denise Scott Brown, *Venturi and Rauch, Architects and Planners, Philadelphia, Pennsylvania*

Hermann H. Field, *Department of Political Science, Tufts University, Medford, Massachusetts*

Reginald G. Golledge, *Department of Geography, The Ohio State University, Columbus, Ohio*

William H. Ittelson, *Environmental Psychology Program, and Center for Research in Cognition and Affect, Graduate Center, City University of New York, New York, New York*

Steven Izenour, *Venturi and Rauch, Architects and Planners, Philadelphia, Pennsylvania*

Joel Kameron, *Environmental Psychology Program, Graduate Center, City University of New York, New York, New York and School of Human Environment, Ramapo College of New Jersey, Mahwah, New Jersey*

Stanley Milgram, *Department of Psychology, Graduate Center, City University of New York, New York, New York*

Harold M. Proshansky, *Environmental Psychology Program, Graduate Center, City University of New York, New York, New York*

Thomas F. Saarinen, *Department of Geography and Area Development, University of Arizona, Tucson, Arizona*

Robert Venturi, *Venturi and Rauch, Architects and Planners, Philadelphia, Pennsylvania*

Gary Winkel, *Environmental Psychology Program, Graduate Center, City University of New York, New York, New York*

Georgia Zannaras, *Department of Geography, The Ohio State University, Columbus, Ohio*

Preface

In recent years, interest in the relationship between environment and a variety of psychological processes has been steadily growing. A rather broadly defined field of environmental psychology, which takes as its subject matter the entire range of psychological phenomena in direct relationship to the large-scale environment, is gradually developing. Problems of definition and of continuity with traditional psychological studies constitute a major issue in this emerging field of investigation. Perhaps nowhere else are these questions more salient than in the study of environment perception and cognition. The breakdown of classical categories of psychological functions—perception, cognition, memory, etc.—which is increasingly characteristic of contemporary psychology is inescapable when we deal with these functions on an environmental scale. Further complicating the work of the student of environment perception and cognition is the fact that until quite recently psychologists have not, with few exceptions, been actively interested in this topic. The gap has been filled by researchers from a variety of other disciplines: Architects, planners, and designers, in addition to other social scientists, have provided a large literature in this area, with rather little concern for adhering to traditional modes of psychological inquiry. The psychologist today finds himself with a large and fascinating literature in the field which lies outside his usual professional readings. The nonpsychologist actively working in the area finds himself, to a very great extent, using psychological procedures and principles with which he may be only passingly acquainted.

This volume represents the first attempt to bridge this gap and to open a dialogue among the various disciplines concerned with problems of environment perception and cognition. Although all disciplines working in this field are not represented, the major areas of geography, psychology, and architecture are. Of the major chapters—written by two psychologists, two geographers, and two architects—those written by the nonpsychologists are provided with introductions by a psychologist. In this way, an attempt is made to maintain the interdisciplinary flavor of the field and, at the same time, to give an overall psychological direction to the volume.

The material presented here represents an edited version of papers originally presented at a conference on Environment and Cognition, held at the Graduate Center of the City University of New York in 1971. The conference was jointly sponsored by the Center for Research in Cognition and Affect and by the Environmental Psychology Program, both of the City University of New York. The conference itself represented the fourth annual conference sponsored by the Center for Research in Cognition and Affect on topics broadly covered by that designation. Earlier conferences were devoted to cognition and affect (Antrobus, 1970), aggression (Singer, 1970), and imagery (Segal, 1971). The Environmental Psychology Program joined in the conference as part of its ongoing training program of students in environmental psychology. The conference was in part supported by U.S. Public Health Service Training Grant MH12441-02 from the National Institute of Mental Health.

I should like to take this opportunity to thank all the contributors to this volume who are the central reason for its coming into being. The Director of the Center, Jerome L. Singer, was enormously helpful in working out the details, both of the conference and of the publication. Beth Merritt, Administrative Assistant in the Environmental Psychology Program, took care of the countless details always encountered in such an operation. Finally, the endless, detailed work of editing all the material presented was efficiently and cheerfully carried out by Natalia Krawetz. To all of these people, I wish to extend my thanks and acknowledge my indebtedness.

Chapter 1

Environment Perception and Contemporary Perceptual Theory

WILLIAM H. ITTELSON[1]
ENVIRONMENTAL PSYCHOLOGY PROGRAM
GRADUATE CENTER
CITY UNIVERSITY OF NEW YORK

The study of perception has been called the weather vane of psychology, suggesting that it points the direction in which future studies in other fields will follow. None of us is likely to quarrel with the assignment of perception to such a central position, if we pause for a moment to consider the role that perception plays in our lives. Cultural as well as individual existence depends on perceiving, and modes of thinking about perceiving are central in setting the intellectual climate of any time. In fact, to be alive is to be sentient. If we did not perceive, each one of us would be alone in a deeply profound sense of the term, if indeed we could be considered to exist at all. In a word, the study of perception touches on the very essence of human existence.

Periods of turmoil in human thought are likely to be accompanied by periods of reassessment of ideas about perception. Psychology is in such a period today. Consider the contrast with an earlier, but not too distant, time. One hundred years ago, Helmholtz (1962) wrote the *Treatise on Physiological*

[1] Portions of this article have previously appeared, in somewhat modified form, in *Transactions of the New York Academy of Sciences,* 1970, **32** (7), 807-815, Series II.

Optics, that magnificent summary and systematization of all that was known of visual perception. In 1878, he delivered his famous address on the "Facts of Perception" (1968). Of perhaps greater significance than the context of these summary works, is the fact that a single man wrote them. Today no one man would be so foolhardy as to undertake a similar endeavor. This might be dismissed as merely a reflection of the so-called information explosion, with its implication that the Renaissance man is forever gone, and that today no single mind can encompass all there is to know about any subject. Or perhaps it has no deeper significance beyond the self-evident fact that there are no Helmholtzes around today. However, there are men of great intellect working in the field of perception at present, and knowledge has not passed the limits of one man's comprehension. Thus, in all probability there is something more fundamental at issue.

The study of perception has become fragmented into a number of loosely connected subproblems which cannot, as presently formulated, be joined together into a larger whole. We may speculate briefly as to some of the historical reasons for this particular research strategy. The atomistic and structuralist psychology of the 19th century, developed in the image of a then universally successful Newtonian atomism, had no alternative. The study of irreducible elements and the laws of their combination was the only acceptable scientific strategy, and the context within which these laws were derived was ruled out as containing any relevance, other than experimental contamination. In the Gestalt reaction, with its explicit interest in the behavioral environment and its recognition of the importance of context, one had the possibility of a study which might truly be called environment perception. That this did not occur is traceable to certain assumptions at the heart of the Gestalt approach. Perception was seen as a single, unitary, and immediate response of a nervous system whose complete workings could be elucidated in any specific example. The same principles of perception would apply in every individual case. While these presuppositions would not necessarily rule out the study of environment perception, the historical fact is that Gestalt perceptual theory was primarily developed through the study of form and object perception.

Over the same period of history, that is, the past half century, a strong current has also been running in the opposite direction. Paradoxically, this has had the same effect of eliminating the larger environmental context as subject matter for perceptual investigation. This trend has been characterized by a strong antimentalistic approach which has tended to rule out as proper subjects for study most of the more fascinating and more complex problems which arise in the larger context. At the same time, the extremely narrow definition of behavior and rigid concept of experimental procedures characteristic of this approach has driven the study of perception almost exclusively into the highly contrived laboratory situation, where object perception is virtually the only avenue open for study.

Thus, in the history of experimental psychology the overwhelming bulk of perception research has been carried out in the context of object perception, rather than environment perception, with the findings of the former providing the basis for understanding the latter. Virtually every major school of psychology in the past 100 years has investigated its perception problems in the context of object perception; has developed its theory of perception from the results of these studies; and has then transferred the explanatory system thus derived into the context of environment perception. As a result, the investigation of perception has lost the essential esthetic unity without which any pursuit leads to chaos, rather than resolution.

When all the historical trends are taken into account, there still remains an explanatory gap which can be accounted for only by paraphrasing Whitehead's famous comment, that it takes an uncommon mind to undertake the study of the obvious. There is nothing more obvious than the environment, and with few exceptions psychologists have not possessed minds uncommon enough to undertake its study. However, the revolution in perceptual studies, which took form in the postwar decade and has accelerated with such remarkable consequences in the past 5 or 10 years, has demonstrated the inadequacy of the old assumptions and has pointed out clear trends for future work. The unity which is needed in the study of perception will be accomplished in psychology only if its concepts of the nature of the environment and man's role in it are reconsidered. Thus, psychologists need to reexamine carefully what is meant by perception and its role in the overall functioning of the individual.

Perceiving is both phenomenal experience and directive for action. Both aspects are crucial. Until quite recently, students of perception have been guided by Aristotle and have approached perception as the conscious experience of sensory input. But perceiving is actually a much more complex process. If this suggestion were offered as mere personal evaluation, it would be neither very startling, nor very helpful. However, the complexity of perceiving stands as one of the most important empirical findings of contemporary work.

The adjective "complex" is not used here to mean extremely complicated and difficult to understand, although these qualities are certainly true of perception. Such a statement would scarcely qualify as a great new insight and certainly would not present major obstacles. Nor is "complex" used in the quantitative sense of having numerous components, although, again, this is quite true of perception and strikes somewhat closer to the intended meaning. Certainly the number of separate and unique perceptual situations one individual encounters in a lifetime is huge, of the order of magnitude of the number of waking seconds in his life. But this staggering quantitative complexity is not, in and of itself, a source of great difficulty. Within the framework of a few general principles, divers special cases can be encompassed: That is one of the central features of science—one of the foundations of its strength. The need for reassessing the understanding of the complexities of the problem arises precisely because general explanatory principles for perception have not been found. It is not the magnitude of the complexity which has not been grasped, but rather the nature of the complexity—to borrow a term from Chomsky (1968), the quality of the complexity. That is, the quality of the explanatory systems used has not matched the quality of the phenomenon to be explained. It is not that perception is too complex; it is, rather, that perception is complex in a different way.

If perception, considered as experience, is complex, so is it complex when viewed as directive for action. An understanding of the total environmental network within which perceiving takes place, both as a source of information and as an arena for action, is an essential first step in unraveling this complexity.

Every organism lives out its day in relation to, and as part of, a larger environmental context. All but the most primitive organisms receive information from this context through sense organs and process it, together with information from other sources, in a nervous system. The reception and processing of information from the environment constitutes the area of study designated as perception. Even within the narrow confines of experimental psychology the problem has been formulated in many ways and has been studied using diverse methodologies. But whatever the specifics of their approach, all investigators recognize, sometimes explicitly, but more frequently implicitly, that perception is important as an area of study because it is the source of information about the environment—which is intimately related to the adaptive functioning of the organism.

To start with a teleological question: Why do organisms have sensory receptors? This question can be translated into more acceptably scientific formulations. From an evolutionary perspective, the question is: What adaptive advantages accrue from the possession of sensory receptors? In psychological terminology one might ask: What is the function of sensory reception in the total behavior of the organism?

The answers to these questions become important because they determine, to a very large extent, the way in which the problem of perception is formulated, and the variables which are considered relevant to this problem. For example, considered from an evolutionary point of view, it is evident that the reception, the transformation, and the utilization of stimuli from the environment cannot be separated. It is true that in a limited sense one can study the receptor mechanisms and the response mechanisms independently. However, to understand any specific instance, we must know the interrelationships among the receptor potentials, the response repertoire, and the environmental opportunities.

The very fact that a particular organism has survived presupposes some degree of compatibility among these three features. We rarely, if ever, find receptor capabilities far beyond the response potentials of the organism. Similarly, the response repertoire of the organism is geared to the particular range of environmental stimuli with regard to which the receptor provides information. Simpson has suggested that if a protozoa were to receive an image by its sensory apparatus it is, so to speak, difficult to see what it could do about this. Following this lead one can ask: Would a theory of perception of the protozoa have to be significantly modified if the protozoa were suddenly granted an image-forming eye? If the answer to this question is no, as indeed it must be, at least one particularly far reaching implication follows: An adequate theory of perception must be, to a certain extent, specific to the particular organism being examined.

As one considers different levels of evolutionary development, there are certain well-established trends relevant to the discussion—the increased modifiability of processes, the difference between fixed receptor–response sequences and "data processing" mechanisms for handling receptor information, the number of other processes interrelated to the particular one being considered, and the areas of functioning relevant to the particular process. These trends, although developing at different rates, tend to be common characteristics of the growing complexity of the total organism. In man, increased freedom from fixed sensory-motor pathways has made the interrelationship among diverse psychological functions increasingly more possible.

At lower levels, sensory reception is limited largely to the avoidance of noxious situations and the approach to nurturant ones. As organisms grow more complex, sensory reception enters into many other functions: distance reception, identification, communication, sexual attraction, and more complex social interrelationships. In man, this trend is accentuated and perception, in addition to these functions, acquires relevance to many other processes far removed from the adaptive significances observable at lower levels—for example, language and esthetic experience.

Furthermore, the predictive function of perception becomes quite explicit. A quarter of a century ago, Ames (Cantril, 1960) recognized this in describing perceptions as "prognostic directives for action." Bruner (1970) has more recently noted that:

> What holds together the structure of sensory organization and the structure of action is, in effect, a signalling of intended action, against which the feedback of the senses during action is compared in order to provide discrepance information and the basis of correction. There is now much evidence that biological systems do in fact operate in some manner close to this [p. 83].

One characteristic which the evolutionary and the psychological questions have in common is their focus on the relationship between perception and the external environment. The evolutionary implication that this relationship must in some sense be adaptive is related to the psychological implication that the relationship has something to do with the behavior of the organism. In very general terms, one fundamental feature of perceiving is that it is relevant or appropriate to the situation in which it occurs. While few would be inclined to argue with this statement, differences emerge as soon as attempts are made to specify what is meant by relevancy or appropriateness.

In psychology, these terms have traditionally been translated to mean accuracy or correctness considered as a match between reality and appearance. This view is also the everyday, common sense view. Yet it is deeply rooted in experimental psychology as exemplified by Wundt (1912), its founder, who wrote, "for every piece of knowledge two factors are necessary—the subject who knows and the object known, independent of this subject [p. 197]."

In contrast, Whitehead (1957) has written that "we must not slip into the fallacy of assuming that we are comparing a given world with given perceptions of it [p. 47]." Bridgman adds "that it is in fact meaningless to try to separate observer and observed, or to speak of an object independent of an observer, or, for that matter, of an observer in the absence of objects of observation [1954, p. 37]."

The relative philosophical adequacy of these contrasting formulations is a matter of continuing debate. Suffice it to say that most experimental studies of perception use the traditional criterion for assessing relevance to the situation—the comparison of a psychological response with a physical measure. Whether this procedure is useful, and indeed whether it is philosophically sound, is a function of its appropriateness to the problem, and not of the method itself. The intention here is not to examine the vast body of work in which this criterion has been used, but rather to suggest that there are other criteria for assessing relevancy of perceiving to a situation—criteria which have come to be recognized as at least equally valid, and perhaps applicable to other classes of phenomena.

One such criterion is that of consensual validation. The appeal to the consensus of a large group of equally involved individuals is perhaps the most frequently used criterion of relevancy. What everyone agrees upon is considered relevant, and deviations from this become irrelevant or inappropriate. The consensus is usually, though not necessarily, made explicit through verbal statements with phenomenological referents. The criterion of consensual validation is increasingly important as the situation becomes increasingly complex. If, on the one hand, I wish to study the apparent size of a piece of paper, I can usefully resort to comparisons with physical measurements. If, on the other hand, I am interested in the sense of size of a room, what the architects call its scale, I find some form of consensual validation the only useful criterion to apply.

There are still other types of problems and situations in which a third criterion of relevancy must be applied. Indeed, the most obvious and common sense approach to the question is the pragmatic one. Is behavior effective? Is it adaptive to the situation? If so, then the perception can be labeled appropriate. However, the pragmatic criterion implies some knowledge of the goal, or intent, of the perceiver. Here lies the difficulty in applying this seemingly self-evident test. The predictive function of perception is thus central to any pragmatic approach to perceptual relevance. Effectiveness can be evaluated only in term of intent, which raises extremely difficult problems.

There are, then, at least three useful criteria for assessing the appropriateness of perception to the situation. One can compare some identifiable aspect of the response to some identifiable physical characteristic of the situation; one can compare the response of one individual to the responses of others in the same situation; one can evaluate the effectiveness of behavior in the situation. An examination of these three criteria for relevancy suggests two conclusions: first, that relevancy has no meaning apart from the criteria used to evaluate it; and second, that the applicable criteria will vary from situation to situation, and from problem to problem.

There is, however, in addition to the procedures just discussed, a quite different direction from which experimental psychology has approached the question of the relation between perceiving and the situation; namely the role of the stimulus. Here the traditional position has been to assert the complete control of the stimulus over psychological events.

Instead of examining the history or the evidence concerning this belief, I shall simply assert that the notion of perceiving being relatively free from control by the external stimulus is an inescapable conclusion at present. From the viewpoint of the perceptual theorist, this means that perception cannot be understood by reference to the stimulus alone. On the face of it, this represents an unbelievable state of affairs regarding a process which, for millenia, has been thought of in terms of the direct consequences of sensory stimulation. And yet, the relative independence of perceiving from the stimulus is one of the most remarkable conclusions of contemporary studies.

Note, however, that freedom from stimulus control does not imply that the stimulus is in no way involved in the perceptual process. Clearly it is. It would be difficult to find a writer who claims otherwise. The questions are, rather, how the stimulus has come to be defined and what its role is seen to be. Traditionally in psychology the stimulus has had a very specific and limited meaning. It is physical energy outside the organism which, when it impinges on the organism, initiates processes, the end product of which is a response wholly determined, and predictable from the nature of the stimulus. This may be an oversimplification, but it is not a distortion. It is certainly what Stevens (1966) meant when he said that "there is only one problem in all of psychology—the definition of the stimulus [p. 31]."

The evidence against a stimulus determination approach to perception has accumulated slowly and from many directions. In the years immediately following World War II, this work began with great fanfare; and while the rejection of a stimulus determination approach has not taken place suddenly or dramatically, it is virtually complete.

The intention here is not to catalog evidence leading to the change in conceptualization of "stimulus." However, a rather subtle change in terminology which has been gradually manifesting itself illustrates the fact that the change has indeed taken place. Today one regularly encounters references to "stimulus information" in contexts where "stimulus" would have been used in the very recent past. Gibson (1966), for example, has devoted most of his recent book to spelling out his notion of stimulus information. Contrast, for example, the statement made in 1950 that, "the term 'stimulus' will always refer to the light change on the retina [p. 63]," with his affirmation in 1966 that this kind of definition "fails to distinguish between stimulus *energy* and stimulus *information* and this difference is crucial [p. 29]."

The concept of stimulus information is not always carefully defined and explicitly stated. "The first problem in the study of visual perception is the discovery of the stimulus [p. 204]," Neisser wrote (1968). A comfortable traditional view, one thinks. He then asked, "What properties of the incoming optic array are informative for vision [p. 204]?" The concept of stimulus turns out to be obliquely, but nonetheless firmly, tied to the concept of information. One could multiply examples. At present, the term "stimulus information" is at best a loose one, with probably as many uses as there are writers. Conceptual clarification and agreement will come as the concept proves its value; here the fact that the terminology has gained widespread use is itself sufficient.

The stimulus considered as a source of information, then, is quite a different proposition from the stimulus considered as a source of stimulation. For one thing, stimulation can be understood in the immediate context of physical and physiological reactions: Information refers to a much larger context. The stimulus information referred to by students of perception is information from, and about, the environment within which the individual lives and functions. This position was made quite explicit 30 years ago by Tolman and Brunswik (1935) when they put forth the notion of environmental probabilities. For Brunswik (1956), as he later amplified his views, the information coming from the environment is never perfectly correlated with the source of the information, that is, some information is more valid than other information. The process of extracting information from the environment thus also involves the extraction of the probability factors or validity coefficients of the information. Similarly, Gibson (1966), today, although differing in almost every detail, is emphatic in asserting the same underlying postulate, that a detailed understanding of the environment as a source of information is an essential and necessary part of the study of perception. Many other writers, spanning both the temporal and the conceptual distance between these two, attest to the interest of students of perception in the total environmental context within which the perceiver functions. For example, one consequence of what might be called the environment corollary of the stimulus-information hypothesis, is the prediction that environments which differ in significant ways will lead to perceivers who perceive in significantly different ways. Considerable experimental effort in recent years has been devoted to examining this proposition, with generally affirmative results. Most important, the studies have strengthened, rather than weakened, acceptance of the importance of the environmental context as a source of stimulus information.

Consider the studies using environments which differ naturally—as in cross-cultural studies of perception (Allport & Pettigrew, 1957; Segall, Campbell, & Herskovits, 1966), or artificially—as in the long series of studies using distorting lenses of various kinds (Rock, 1966).

A second consequence of the stimulus information hypothesis has been the gradual breakdown of the traditional, conceptual compartmentalization of the various, so-called basic psychological processes. Stimuli considered as stimulation are quite specific. This statement reached its classic expression in the specific energy of nerves which provided the final link in an apparently immutable sequence. Light stimulates photoreceptors; photoreceptors stimulate optic nerves; optic nerves produce visual experience. This, and no other sequence is allowable to the student of perception. The concept of stimulus information is one of many influences which have led to a reevaluation of the traditional approach. Information is nonspecific with regard to the channel through which it is transmitted, the form, or locus of its storage.

The power of the information concept lies in the generality of information. At most, one may postulate that information can enter the system from various sources; but once in the system, one unit of information is fully on par with all other units. For example, a narrow definition of "visual information" has no place in such a system and is replaced by a broader notion of all information which has relevance to visual perception. This latter is both theoretically and empirically shown to be a much larger category. The result has been a breakdown of the rigid compartmentalization of psychological processes and a recognition that many processes which had previously been sharply distinguished from perception are, in fact, concurrently and actively involved in every act of perceiving.

The study of the relationship between perception and cognition can serve as an illustration. For a sizable part of its history, psychology, with few exceptions, handled this problem by refusing to recognize its existence. Perception was studied from the standpoint of what one might call, with some license, the external mechanics of the process according to the stimulus-determination tradition. Insofar as cognition was considered in relation to perception, it was summed up by the ancient dictum, "seeing is believing." The road to the cognitive or belief system lay through the perceptual process.

Approximately two decades ago psychology, in a burst of self-conscious sophistication, challenged the wisdom of the ages and rewrote that law. "Believing is seeing" became the keynote of a generation of perceptual studies. No longer did perception mirror an external world which we believed precisely because we saw it. On the contrary, perception mirrored our innermost values and produced a world which we saw precisely because we believed in it. Today, of course, it is known that neither of these views is correct because both are predicated on the inadequate assumption that two separate and isolated systems are involved–perception and cognition, with certain fixed and unidirectional contacts between them.

A large body of work has led to a growing acceptance of an approach which considers the whole perceptiocognitive system as part of a larger system whose fundamental function is the processing of information. More and more activities formerly considered to be exclusively the province of cognitive functioning are being shown to be inseparably a part of perceiving as well. What used to be considered simple sensory discriminations are now considered in detection theory to involve complex judgments subtly influenced by such apparent features as the individual's value hierarchy. Or consider from another point of view, continuing studies of the reticular system show the involvement, even in a direct sensory level, of such previously considered remote processes as attention and concomitant needs.

Perhaps nowhere is the interconnection between perceiving and other psychological processes more clearly shown than in relationship to memory. Some of the examples of this interrelationship do not correspond to the common sense, everyday concept of memory. The term is used here in the very general sense of the storage and later utilization of information. Two general types of memory have been studied in connection with perceiving: long-term and short-term memory, each of which operates in a quite different way from the other. Within each of these categories, two subtypes of memory have been revealed: one involved in the processing of visual information, and the other in the retention of visual information. Whether these distinctions will hold up with further study, or will prove to be merely different ways of looking at a single process, we cannot yet know. However, the four roles of memory are easily illustrated.

The function of short-term memory in the processing of visual information is immediately suggested by the fact that our perceptual experience has a form, a structure, and a continuity over time. Discrete and erratic sensory input emerges as continuous and ordered perception. Even more compelling evidence is provided by experiments which demonstrate that sequences presented over fairly long periods of time, in the order of seconds, determine the nature of the immediate perceptual experience. Short-term memory thus provides not only a continuity of perception, but also a continuous monitoring of the actual processing of information.

Long-term memory in the processing of visual information leads into an area which has probably been mislabeled "perceptual learning." It is clear that there are long-term changes over time in the ways whereby perceptual information is processed. The role of the environment as a source of information and the acquisition over time of this information has already been noted. Perceptual adaptation, sensory deprivation, and a variety of other procedures can probably all be subsumed in this general context. Perceptual experience, in short, has been shown to influence, in a variety of ways, the later processing of perceptual information.

The direct retention of perceptual information is less clearly differentiated into two different processes involving short-term and long-term memory; but in the extremes, the differences are quite clear—short-term memory might be termed "photographic," and long-term memory, "symbolic." The distinction between these processes, as well as the confusion between them, is well illustrated by studies in the memory of color. If, for example, a color is presented and the subject is asked immediately afterward to match it from a color chart, he can typically do so almost as if the color were still in front of him. However, if an extended period of time elapses after showing the color, the subject can, in general, match it only if he has already provided himself with a symbolic label or name for the color. These distinctions are obscured, however, by the possibility of long-term eidetic imagery, a subject in need of further study.

This telescoped summary of relationships between perception and memory reiterates that the distinction between what formerly had been considered separate and discrete processes is arbitrary and archaic. At the one extreme, perception and memory are, if not synonymous, at least equivalent and necessary components of the same process; while at the other extreme, perceptual memory and symbolic processes are inextricably interwoven. The precarious state of memory as a separate psychological process was noted by Kiss (1971) who, in reviewing a book on the subject, suggested that it may be the last.

If all that has been said to this point is to be taken seriously, three very general conclusions can be offered on the nature of perceiving. First, perceiving is relatively free from direct control by the stimulus. Second, it is inseparably linked to, and indeed indistinguishable from, other aspects of psychological functioning. Third, and perhaps paradoxically, perceiving is relevant and appropriate to the environmental context in which it occurs.

The foregoing discussion points to the necessity of considering the environment as a subject for perceptual studies, while at the same time suggesting why this topic has been largely neglected. This neglect has even been apparent in studies logically quite close to the environment, such as space perception. The space studied in traditional space perception is quite different from the environment as considered in the present context. Most space perception is in fact concerned quite explicitly with objects in space, their distance, orientation, movement, and the like. Space perception, as usually conceived, and in spite of its name, is closely linked to the more obviously object-oriented approaches.

The distinction between object and environment is crucial. Objects require subjects—a truism whether one is concerned with the philosophical unity of the subject–object duo, or is thinking more naively of the object as a "thing" which becomes a matter for psychological study only when observed by a subject. In contrast, one cannot be a subject of an environment, one can only be a participant. The very distinction between self and nonself breaks down: the environment surrounds, enfolds, engulfs, and no thing and no one can be isolated and identified as standing outside of, and apart from, it.

Environments surround. Perhaps that statement says no more than the dictionary has already told us. Nevertheless, it will be considered more closely, after first looking at the question of scale. Perceptual objects may be very large in scale; anyone who has flown over Manhattan Island on one of its rare clear days knows that Manhattan can be a beautiful object indeed. But object it is under these conditions, apart from, and observed by, the subject. Environments are necessarily larger than that which they surround, and the environments under discussion here are large in relation to man. In a very general way this means large enough to permit, and indeed require, movement in order to encounter all aspects of the situation—at least the size of a small room and generally much larger. (Telephone booths, elevators, closets, or even automobiles and space capsules are environments, but one intuitively senses that they are special cases and perhaps involve different processes than do larger environmental contexts.) Large-scale environments, extending from rooms through houses, neighborhoods, cities, countrysides, to the whole universe in size, necessarily possess many properties which objects almost always do not, and usually cannot, have. And these characteristics, to a large extent, determine the nature of the problem posed by environment perception.

The quality of surrounding—the first, most obvious, and defining property—forces the observer to become a participant. One does not, indeed cannot, observe the environment: one explores it. If the observation is the object, then the exploration is the environment. The problem of exploratory behavior, its nature, function, and its relation to the individual's larger purposes, becomes central to the study of environment perception. The limits of the exploration, moreover, are not determined; the environment has no fixed boundaries in space or time, and one must study how the explorer himself goes about setting boundaries to the various environments he encounters. The exploratory aspects of environment perception can thus extend over large spaces and long time spans, and require some process of spatial and temporal summation; both long- and short-term memory are essential.

Environments, in additon, are always multimodal. It may be possible to conceive of an environment which offers information through only one sense modality, but it probably would be impossible to build. In any event, it would be a curiosity. Perceptual experiments have been notably deficient in their study of multimodal processes, and yet these are essential for understanding environment perception. We need to know the relative importance of the various modalities, the kinds of environmental concepts, and sets of environmental predictabilities associated with each modality. But more important, we need to know how they function in concert: what processes are involved when supplementing, conflicting, and distracting information is presented through several modalities at once.

A third necessary characteristic of environments is that peripheral, as well as central, information is always present, peripheral in the mechanical sense—the area behind one is no less a part of the environment than that in front—and peripheral in the sense of being outside the focus of attention. Both meanings are important and raise questions concerning the processes underlying the direction of attention.

Fourth, environments always provide more information than can possibly be processed. Questions of channel capacity and overload are inherent in environmental studies. However, the mere quantity of information does not tell the whole story. Environments always represent simultaneously, instances of redundant information, of inadequate and ambiguous information, and of conflicting and contradictory information. The entire mechanism of information processing in the nervous system, about which psychologists are only beginning to learn, is brought into play.

The four characteristics of environments which objects either cannot or usually do not possess (their surrounding quality; their multimodal property; the presence of peripheral stimulation; and the presence of too much information which is simultaneously redundant, inadequate, and contradictory) already suggests that findings in object perception can be applied only with great caution to environment perception. But these characteristics are nevertheless, rather traditional in perceptual studies in that they refer to what can very broadly be called stimulus properties. Beyond these properties, however, there is another group of properties of the environment which must be taken into account in any study of environment perception, and which are almost completely foreign to the field of object perception.

The first of these, or a fifth characteristic of the environment, is that environment perception always involves action. Environments, as we have seen, are not and cannot be passively observed; they provide the arena for action. They define the probabilities of occurrence of potential actions, they demand qualities which call forth certain kinds of actions, and they offer differing opportunities for the control and manipulation of the environment itself.

Environments call forth actions, but not blind, purposeless actions. Of course, what an individual does can be expected to be largely influenced by the particular purposes which he brings to the situation; at the same time, however, the environment possesses the property, a sixth characteristic, of providing symbolic meanings and motivational messages which themselves may affect the directions which action takes. Meanings and motivational messages are a necessary part of the content of environment perception.

Finally, and perhaps most important of all, environments always have an ambiance, an atmosphere, difficult to define, but overriding in importance. One can at this point only speculate on some of the features of the environment which contribute to this ambiance and which, thereby, become of central significance for the study of environment perception. First of all, environments are almost without exception encountered as part of a social activity; other people are always a part of the situation and environment perception is largely a social phenomenon. Second, environments always have a definite esthetic quality. Esthetically neutral objects can be designed; esthetically neutral environments are unthinkable. Last, environments always have a systemic quality. The various components and events relate to each other in particular ways which, perhaps more than anything else, serve to characterize and define the particular environment. The identification of these systemic relationships is one of the major features of the process of environment perception.

Thus, to the first four characteristics dealing roughly with stimulus properties, three others must be added: the role of action and purpose as defined, delimited, and called forth by the environment; the presence of meanings and motivational messages carried by the environment; and the concept of ambiance, related to the esthetic, social, and systemic qualities of the environment. This list represents a minimum set of considerations which must be taken into account in any adequate study of environment perception. But how is this to be accomplished? The separate study of the various processes in isolation is likely to yield a sum substantially smaller than the whole it seeks to explain, and a more fruitful approach is likely to involve investigations carried out in the context of the full-scale environment. That is, one can either make use of already existing environments and/or construct experimental environments.

The existing, everyday environment has, of course, the advantages of being readily available, obviously relevant, and usually inexpensive to study. It has the disadvantage of being approached by the participant with a vast amount of information already in hand, which may serve to mask important aspects of the process involved in the acquiring of that information. The novel environment, particularly the constructed laboratory environment, has the disadvantages of seeming unreal and contrived, as well as being quite expensive. Yet to the extent that it is in fact novel, it can elucidate the process of acquiring information in ways which cannot be accomplished in familiar surroundings. Unfortunately, experimental environments for the study of environment perception have so far been almost nonexistent.

The perception of the everyday environment, in contrast, has been studied by a number of investigators, principally geographers, architects, and others outside the field of psychology. They have undertaken the study of mental maps of large environments, the identification of salient characteristics contributing to one's awareness of the city, and the analysis of meanings attributed to specific environmental contexts, for example. The general aim of these studies is to identify environmental search, or exploratory strategies, and the cognitive strategies used in conceptualizing the environment, with the ultimate aim of developing a comprehensive theory of the acquisition and utilization of information about environmental systems and subsystems.

Answers to these questions will be long in coming, but some findings, tentative and preliminary to be sure, are available which do command some degree of confidence. Most immediately obvious is the evidence of individual differences. But regardless of individual differences, people seem to organize perceptual responses to the environment around five identifiable and interrelated levels of analysis. These are: affect, orientation, categorization, systematization, and manipulation. The comments which follow about each of these levels are quite general; the details need further study and will vary with the nature of both the physical situation and the social relationships involved.

The first level of response to the environment is affective. The direct emotional impact of the situation, perhaps largely a global response to the ambiance, very generally governs the directions taken by subsequent relations with the environment. It sets the motivational tone and delimits the kinds of experiences one expects and seeks. The importance of the immediate affective response is sharply etched in the novel environment; it can be seen in the laboratory, the city, the school, and the hospital. It is gradually blurred and glossed over by familiarity, but its consequences are indelible.

The establishment of orientation within the environment is a second level of response. The identification of escape routes is perhaps the most primitive form of orientation and is particularly compelling in novel environments with negative affect. Generally the location of positive and negative features, including other people, result in an initial mapping of the situation which provides a base for more detailed exploration.

Along with a satisfactory level of orientation, the process of developing categories for analysis and understanding is undertaken; the first steps are made toward developing a taxonomy which in a sense is never to be completed. The initial categories probably have to do with events from which objects are ultimately distilled in more and more detail. The process of concept formation and the nature of conceptual categories require careful study in this context. It is already known that conceptual categories are not imposed by the external situation, but are largely governed by goals, predispositions, and generalized expectations which the individual has already internalized. The path to unique and idiosyncratic categories is open.

A fourth level in the process of environment perception is the systematic analysis of relationships within the environment. Predictable sequences of events are identified and separated from random or unique occurrences. Causal connections are postulated and verified. The complex set of interrelationships which characterizes any particular environment is gradually brought into order and harmony. This order, or system, in the environment is analogous to constancy in objects. Properties of the system remain constant in the presence of continually changing events, in much the same way that properties of objects remain constant in spite of ever-changing stimulation. Or perhaps it may prove more correct to say that object constancy is a special case derived from the more general continuity of the environmental system.

Throughout this process the individual is never passive. He acts within, and as part of, the situation. He learns both the kinds of interventions he can bring about and their consequences, generally in terms of environmental change and, more important, in relation to his own needs and purposes. In this context, the relevance of perception to the situation in which it occurs can be defined for the individual as the mutually supporting construction of action and perception in the service of purpose.

Affect, orientation, categorization, systematization, and manipulation are the processes involved in environment perception. They do not function sequentially, but continuously interact with each other. Each aspect calls for its own set of strategies which are probably characteristic of the individual. The identification and study of these strategies is just beginning, and any statements are speculative. However, it does seem clear that the individual cannot be separated from the environment. He is part of the system he is perceiving, and the strategies he chooses become part of the environment he in turn experiences as being external to himself.

The way one views the environment thus is, in a very general sense, a function of what one does in it, including what strategies are used in exploring and conceptualizing it. And what is done in the environment represents, in turn, a choice among many alternatives, the nature and scope of which are progressively restricted by previous, frequently irreversible decisions. It is not unreasonable to say that the environment is experienced the way it is because one chooses to see it that way. In this sense the environment is an artifact created in man's own image.

This approach is clearly in sharp contrast to a "common sense" view which dichotomizes the situation into man and environment and assumes simple, direct, causal sequences: the environment acting on man, or man acting on the environment. In practice these sequences do not exist; and one deals empirically with a situation involving complex interdependencies. In any concrete situation, one does not encounter man and his environment as separate but interacting; instead, one finds a total situation which can be analyzed in a variety of ways. What is environment under one mode of analysis may not be environment under another. The conclusion is reached that the common sense view must be completely reversed. Rather than defining the situation in terms of its components, the components, including man himself, can be defined only in terms of the situation in which they are encountered. Man and his environment are never encountered independently: they are encountered only in a concrete situation, and they can be defined only in terms of their modes of participation within the situation.

The "environment" is thus seen as a total, active, continuous process involving the participation of all aspects. All the components of the environment are defined in terms of their participation in the total process; no component is seen as an entity existing in an environment composed of other entities. Man and his environment are inseparable, and both are defined in terms of their participation in the total environmental process. In any concrete situation, the "environment" has no fixed boundaries in either space or in time. Perhaps the best way of conceptualizing this is to view the environment as an open, rather than a closed, system. Within this system it is clear that the process exhibits stable patterns which resist change and which may be common from one situation to another, and from one time to another. At the same time, the situation is constantly changing. The very participation of the various aspects, or components, of the process produces disequilibria which, in turn, alter the mode of participation of the various aspects and thus change the total environmental situation in a continuing process.

In summary then, the environment involves the active participation of all aspects. Man is never concretely encountered independent of the situation through which he acts, nor is the environment ever encountered independent of the encountering individual. It is meaningless to speak of either as existing apart from the situation in which it is encountered. The word "transaction" has been used to label such a situation, for the word carries a double implication: one, all parts of the situation enter into it as active participants; and two, these parts owe their very existence as encountered in a situation to such active participation—they do not appear as already existing entities which merely interact with each other without affecting their own identity.

The term "transaction" was first used in this general context by Dewey and Bentley (1949) for whom it took on far-reaching philosophical significance. It may be best to close by stating, in their own words, Dewey and Bentley's understanding of this term.

> "Observation of this general [transactional] type sees man in action, not as something radically set over against an environing world nor yet as something merely acting "in" a world, but as action *of* and *in* the world in which man belongs as an integral constituent [p. 52]." Under this procedure we treat "all of [man's] behavings, including his most advanced knowings, as activities not of himself alone, nor even as primarily his, but as processes of the full situation of organism-environment [p. 104]." "From birth to death every human being is a *Party,* so that neither he nor anything done or suffered can possibly be understood when it is separated from the fact of participation in an extensive body of transactions—to which a given human being may contribute and which he modifies, but only in virtue of being a partaker in them [p. 271]."

Chapter ii

Introduction

STANLEY MILGRAM[1]
DEPARTMENT OF PSYCHOLOGY
GRADUATE CENTER
CITY UNIVERSITY OF NEW YORK

In this chapter important questions are raised regarding the relationship of man to his environment. I would like to comment on the issues, introduce a few methodological cautions (a psychologist's birthright), and extend the author's discussion of psychological maps.

Let me start with the study of the Great Plains Farmers. The author uses projective devices to uncover some of the feelings, motives, and conflicts experienced by those inhabiting a particular physical environment. However, there are two critical questions in using any projective device: the first involves the quality of evidence derived from such tests. Placing a picture in front of a subject and asking him to tell a story about it is as good a way as any to start him talking. However, projective devices are better as stimulants than as sources of evidence; they tend to generate rich output, subject to diverse interpretation. For example, Thomas Saarinen detects conflicts in his subjects. However, one needs to ask whether it is necessarily the Great Plains environment which gives rise to such expressions of conflict, or whether these are indicative of other aspects of the farmers' lives and character.

A second critical question concerns the optimal use of various types of tests. Projective tests are useful if they can get at motives, feelings, and emotions which cannot be tapped by more direct means. But there is no value

[1] The author wishes to thank Harriet Weiss for assistance in preparing these comments for publication.

in using such indirect methods of assessment if direct access to feelings and sentiments is equally available. At this point psychologists do not know whether projective tests or direct questioning techniques are more efficient devices for learning about the effects of environment on men. Such explorations as those undertaken by Dr. Saarinen are to be encouraged, without prematurely proclaiming them the optimal tools for the job at hand.

Whatever the limitations of the study, it nonetheless raises a truly intriguing question: *To what degree is the way man thinks, feels, and perceives shaped by variations in his environment?* There are two overall views on this. One holds that man's thought processes are in no way restricted by environment. Consider, for example, that a motley band of Aramaic tribesmen wandering in the deserts of Sinai emerged with universal truths that are appreciated by all of mankind. The other view, typified in Huntington's assertions (1945) about the effects of climate on culture, maintains that entire civilizations are dependent on particular environmental conditions. What could be more challenging an intellectual quest than to understand in what manner man's nature and intellect are shaped by the environment, and in what manner man transcends the environment. Consider the fact that a person living in a desert has relatively few anchoring points in his environment. The dunes shift; to get from one point to the next becomes an intellectual problem. How different a life this must be from one containing stable, impressive, natural, reference points at every turn. It is no accident that trigonometry developed in Arabic mathematics. After all, if a person travels from oasis A to oasis B, he must spend half his trip wondering whether he started off at the correct angle; it may be days before a landmark will confirm his judgment.

In his discussion of mental maps, Dr. Saarinen brings up a major issue: How is the environment represented in men's minds? This leads to a set of more specific questions we can ask about any mental maps.

Units and Distortions

First, what units of the environment are to be mapped? In his discussion, Saarinen goes from campus to world, and as he indicated, one could go on to neighborhood, city, and so forth. But there is an important difference in acquiring a mental map of one's campus and that of the world. The campus map is mediated by direct experience, moving about the university buildings, and piecing together scenes into some cognitive structure. The image of the world is learned not from direct experience with the world, but by formal schemata of it as represented in maps and atlases. For example, Saarinen describes a Finnish boy who drew an exaggerated cartographical representation of Finland. It is not because he saw Finland "large" in the same sense that university students saw their campus. His image of Finland as a total geographical entity was not derived from direct experience. More likely, it came from his familiarity with maps and atlases, which tend to distort the size of countries near the two poles. Under what range of conditions, one may wonder, does direct experience mediate the development of mental maps, and when are more formal schemata utilized?

Returning to the example of the Finnish boy, it is also possible that his exaggerated drawing was influenced partially by the fact that his native land is the geographic area with which he is most familiar. Psychologically, one tends to give most prominence to those objects and events of which one has the most knowledge and awareness. Of course, there may be an actual neural reality to this phenomenon, and not just the expression of local vanities. One is reminded of the homunculus appearing in introductory psychology textbooks in which the parts of the body are shown in a size proportionate to the area of the brain they require. The size distortions in mental maps may in some way represent an amount proportional to the molecular storage units used for different realms of the environment.

Another question to be asked about mental maps is: What happens when there is a clash between the formal schemata and direct experience? Such a phenomenon occurred in history when Christopher Columbus set sail in the Atlantic. Relying on the best cartographical evidence available at the time, Columbus believed that he should arrive at Asia if he sailed west. At first, he thought he had reached China, but the inhabitants were not speaking Chinese. Thus, the view derived from maps conflicted with experience. (He finally concluded, before his death, that he had indeed reached Asia, but instead of China, had sailed upon part of Indonesia whose inhabitants were southeast Asians.)

Even today cartographical distortion produces misguided pictures of the world. Such distortion inevitably results from putting a global map on flat paper. In his discussion, Saarinen uses Mercator maps to illustrate certain points. One distortion of the Mercator map is that Greenland appears much larger than it actually is, so that many people think of it as one of the largest continents. There are also climatic distortions based on the generalized concept that as one approaches the Equator, the weather gets increasingly warmer. This idea has kept many people from going south in the summer to a place such as Mexico City, which, in reality, is quite pleasant because of its high altitude. In subtle ways mental representations of the environment, even when they depart from objective reality, come to influence behavior. In addition to maps and geographic mythology, what other formal schemata used to represent the environment similarly distort one's conception of the world and lead to mistaken conclusions about it?

Dimensions

Once one decides on what units of the environment are to be mapped, which features are of greatest psychological importance? The most basic question is whether a given geographical entity exists at all in the person's informational repertory. If asked to draw a map of Central America, does he include Costa Rica and El Salvador? If asked about New York City neighborhoods, is he aware of the existence of Chelsea and Morningside Heights? Beyond the identification of a particular element on the map is the question of whether the individual knows the geographic position of one entity in relation to another. He may be able to name Chelsea, but not know its position in relation to other neighborhoods. In addition to these purely cognitive features, the individual may possess a set of attitudes or feelings toward different parts of the mapped area. Certain areas may be more attractive than others; some may induce fearfulness and anxiety. In principle, it is possible to map an entire city, block-by-block, in terms of any definable psychological dimension, for example, perceived level of safety–danger.

Externalizing

The major methodological problem in all of this is how to externalize the mental map, that is, how to get it out of the individual's subjective experience and onto paper for public scrutiny. One simple way to do this is to ask a person to draw a map of the area in question, say, a city, showing all of the streets he knows and indicating all of the neighborhoods and landmarks of which he can think. A decade ago, Kevin Lynch (1960) at M.I.T. asked a group of Bostonians to draw a map of Boston. While certain landmarks, such as Paul Revere's house and the Boston Commons, as well as paths linking them, turned out to be widely known, large areas of the city were not represented in typical mental projections. Certain neighborhoods hardly exist in the minds of Bostonians. This again highlights the difference between the cartographer's map and the psychological map. Donald Hooper (1970) informally applied this cognitive mapping technique to New York City with similar results. The psychological representation of New York was found to be localized in downtown landmarks, with much of the city having no cognitive representation at all in the minds of its inhabitants. Similar results appear in Saarinen's study of the campus maps down by the students at the University of Arizona. The buildings along the Central Mall, a highly frequented pathway, are represented more often and with greater detail and clarity than those along less traveled parts of the campus.

Aggregating

Once the map of a single individual has been externalized, the next problem is to aggregate the individual maps into a group map in order to arrive at some general conclusions. However, unique configurations are always difficult to aggregate in any meaningful fashion. One is reminded of the work of a 19th century criminologist who attempted to find the average criminal type by superimposing the photographed faces of many criminals onto a single photographic plate and using the resulting portrait as an ideal, or average, type. Unfortunately, the resulting face was virtually nondescript and resembled no one, criminal or otherwise. The question, then, is: How can individual maps be combined into a group map which would allow some kind of generalization?

Another question with which Saarinen deals is that of group differences. He notes that on the campus maps drawn by the university students, there was a tendency for students from different departments to depict with greater accuracy the buildings where their classes and departmental activities were most frequently held. The surrounding areas of these buildings were also depicted more accurately. In psychological maps of cities, it would be interesting to note whether different subgroups, such as white stockbrokers and ghetto blacks, hold similar mental images of the city. Comparing maps held by the young and the old adds a developmental dimension. What is the process whereby the maps develop in the individual? Which features come first—landmark, directional, or spatial? And how do the maps change with increasing maturity?

Functional Significance

What difference does it make in psychological functioning if a person has a mental map, let us say, that extends only 10 miles from where he lives, as opposed to one that extends to give a picture of the world? Is attitude, mentality, emotion, conceptualization, breadth of vision influenced by the size of the political unit within which one lives?

People talk about an "insular mentality," which is a feeling that one lives in a circumscribed world with few possibilities for exit. What mental adjustment does this "no exit" view entail? To what extent is it influenced by the environment and to what extent by other factors? I lived for a year in Norway, which is a relatively small country. Yet it did not seem small when I lived there: The people were of normal size and maintained normal spatial distances.

Some historians have maintained that the individual's conception of geographic space *does* make a difference in psychological functioning. The frontier hypothesis (Turner, 1893) states that because Americans in the 19th century viewed themselves as living in an unlimited, rather than a finite, environment, this affected the mentality of the country. If a person were not satisfied with where he was, he could go someplace else. There was always room. In contrast, the current, high suicide rate in Berlin may be the result of the perception of having reached the environmental limits, of having come to the "end of the line," with nowhere else to go. The question of whether people see themselves as living in a finite space, or an infinitely expandable one, is quite important. In the last decade, perhaps there has been no more powerful and sobering metaphor than R. Buckminster Fuller's conception of "Spaceship Earth," depicting the finite and exceedingly circumscribed environment of the planet itself.

Applications

Once the mental maps have been obtained and their significance understood for the individual, what application, if any, do they have for the betterment of human society? Saarinen handles this question implicitly by suggesting that future campus plans take into consideration the composite campus image of the student population. On a larger scale, he points out that an analysis of sketch maps of the world might help in averting dangers based on conflicting world images of different cultural groups. It is also possible that city planners, with a knowledge of mental maps, will be able to better arrange cities so that they communicate a sense of place to the individual, help him to orient himself in a new city, and contribute to his esthetic delight.

Although Saarinen approaches the problem from a geographic viewpoint, the areas of his concern and even the manner of his approach are very similar to those of psychologists. Both geographers and psychologists are interested in the same kinds of problems, which suggests that we are dealing with a real, and not merely an academically defined, phenomenon. Perhaps geographers can derive from psychology enhanced sophistication in testing human subjects (psychologists are experts in knowing how to externalize and measure mental processes). From the geographer, we psychologists can gain a sense of scope to move us outside the two-room laboratory into the larger world.

The Use of Projective Techniques in Geographic Research

THOMAS F. SAARINEN
DEPARTMENT OF GEOGRAPHY AND
AREA DEVELOPMENT
UNIVERSITY OF ARIZONA

Since the early 1960s the field of geography has been increasingly exposed to a growing array of psychological techniques. The works of Burton, Kates, and White (1968) and Saarinen (1969) are examples. Geographical journals have printed many articles with a strong behavioral science slant as geographers have sought answers to the question of how man perceives his environment. Among the many psychological tools with which geographers have experimented in recent years are projective techniques. It is to some of these that I would like to turn here.

Geographers have always been concerned with the man–land relationship, but it is only recently that they have deliberately sought out behavioral science methodology to study it from new perspectives. In large part this may be due to the increasing acceptance of the man–milieu model known as cognitive behavioralism. This is the hypothesis that a person reacts to his environment as he perceives and interprets it in light of his previous experience (Sprout & Sprout, 1965). Since the person's actions in relation to the environment are assumed to depend on his perception of environment, it becomes important to find out just how it is perceived. This leads to the distinction between the "real world," which is called the objective or geographic environment, and the subjective environment or psycho-milieu, which depends on what is perceived by the person. Much of the recent interest among geographers in the use of psychological techniques stems from the desire to find ways to measure or describe aspects of this subjective world. Projective techniques are particularly appropriate for this task and I would like to note a few ways in which they have been used by geographers.

Lindzey and Thorpe (1968) group projective techniques into five main categories based on the nature of the response evoked from the subject: association, construction, completion, choice or ordering, and expression. Each of these has been used to some degree in geographic research.

Association techniques depend on the immediate response of the subject to the stimulus. Various word association techniques and the Rorschach test are well-known examples. A version of this technique was applied in geography by Haddon (1960), who had British students write down in short words or phrases the images which came to mind when they thought about the United States, France, South Africa, and Australia. The same technique was included by Cole (1970) as part of a study on the Carioca's view of the world. Cole had a sample of Brazilians living in Rio de Janeiro write down the five features which first occurred to them when they thought of France, the United States, the U.S.S.R., and England.

The construction category requires the subject to go beyond simple association to stimulus and to create, or construct, a more elaborate product such as a story or a picture. The Thematic Apperception Test (TAT) (Murray, 1943) and the Blacky Pictures fall within this category. A modified version of the TAT was applied in some of my own work among Great Plains wheat farmers (Saarinen, 1966). This was done in collaboration with a psychologist, John Sims, and will be discussed in greater detail later (Sims & Saarinen, 1969).

Completion techniques present the subject with some type of incomplete product which he must complete in any manner that he wishes. Among variants of this type are various sentence-completion, story-completion and argument-completion tests, as well as the Rozenzweig Picture-Frustration Study. A modified version of the latter has been tested for geographic research by Barker and Burton (1969). An example used in the modified version of the test is a cartoon panel which depicts two farmers in a drought-stricken field. The remark of one is indicated in the balloon above his head, while the balloon for the other is left blank for the respondent to complete.

Choice, or ordering, techniques require the respondent to choose from a number of alternatives the item or arrangement which fits some specified criterion. The Szondi Test and Picture Arrangement Test are samples from psychology. Several researchers, such as Zannaras (1968) and Metton (1969), have used this type of technique in asking respondents to delimit on a street map the area of their neighborhood. Although individual variations occur in location and extent of neighborhoods outlined, there is generally enough agreement to make reasonable neighborhood identifications possible. A card-sorting technique was employed by Cox and Zannaras (1970) to investigate the cognitive maps of this country held by a group of undergraduates at The Ohio State University. The students were instructed to select for each state of the United States the three states most similar to them, and for a sample of North American cities to follow the same procedure. These data were then used to produce a subjective regionalization of the United States and to suggest some of the criteria used in classifying groups of cities. Gould's (1966) study on place preferences used the states of the United States as building blocks. Students from various parts of the country ranked the individual states in order of residential preference. These data enabled Gould to demonstrate that while there were common elements to all, each region tended to have a home bias.

Expressive techniques are like construction techniques, but typically place as much emphasis on the manner and style in which the product is created, as upon the product itself. The category includes such things as play, drawing, and painting which are often considered therapeutic as well as diagnostic. The most widely used appear to be various human figure-drawing tests. Similar to the human-figure-drawing exercises in having objective norms for comparison with the subjective product, are techniques in which the respondent is asked to draw from memory, on a blank sheet of paper, maps of various areas. Two such studies are discussed in more detail later: one on the image of the University of Arizona campus (Saarinen, 1967); and the other on student views of the world (Saarinen, 1971). (In the first case the respondent may have a comprehensive visual impression of the area and be totally familiar with it. In the second, only conceptual knowledge is possible, for no one knows all of the world.)

My purpose in running through this outline of the main types of projective techniques was to indicate briefly that these ideas have been diffusing into geography in many forms. The samples I have selected to consider at length are simply those which I have applied myself and can therefore discuss in better detail. The three studies which I wish to turn to now have been noted above: the use of the TAT test among Great Plains wheat farmers (Saarinen, 1966); the study of the image of the University of Arizona campus (Saarinen, 1967); and that of the student views of the world (Saarinen, 1971).

The Great Plains study was completed in 1966 at the University of Chicago, where I was a graduate student in the geography department. Previously, a series of studies had been carried out on the factors affecting human occupance of flood plains (Kates, 1964; White, 1964, 1966). From an original concern with mainly physical factors which could not explain the observed patterns, the focus shifted to include attitudes. Eventually the problem became more clearly defined as how people perceive the flood hazard and the way in which this affects their utilization of areas subject to flood. Perception of other natural hazards were studied, including the drought hazard on the Great Plains.

To investigate the perception of the drought hazard on the Great Plains, I selected a series of six study sites in the Central Great Plains. These included two sites in each of three moisture zones ranging from the most humid to most arid margins of the area. At each study site a number of wheat farmers was interviewed and asked to tell stories to a series of TAT cards. In addition to several of the regular set, a few additional cards were used to more directly elicit stories about drought problems (see Figures 1 and 2).

To introduce the reader unfamiliar with the area to the classic Great Plains situation, I would like to quote a story told in response to Figure 2 by a farmer from Barber County, Kansas.

> *Well I'd say this was a scene in Western Kansas in the dirty 30's. Because of the great opportunities in the late 20's and early 30's this farmer moved to the drylands of the High Plains. His first few years were very successful in harvesting good crops and increasing his bank account. Each year more land was plowed up, vegetation destroyed and lack of moisture made a situation perfect for wind erosion. And for the next four or five years the wind blew and the soil drifted and the farmer's bank account and assets were liquidated. And in despair with his hands in his pockets, and his head bent low he started his return to the big city.*

The story succinctly states the region's basic problem. The Great Plains is a semiarid area. In years of good rainfall, good crops are obtained. Farmers are prosperous. They buy new machines. Everyone in the area is optimistic. But bad years come too. A lack of rain leads to a lack of crops. After several years of drought, as in the 1930s, conditions such as those described in the *Grapes of Wrath* (Steinbeck, 1939) occur, the ruined farmers are driven to seek their fortune elsewhere.

U.S.D.A. Photo

Fig. 1. *Drought hazard TAT card.*

U.S.D.A. Photo

Fig. 2. *Drought scene (Card B).*

The stories told by wheat farmers in response to TAT cards have an authentic, earthy flavor and evoke much local color. But they also indicate some of the recurrent themes of the region and provide a means to investigate certain personality traits which may be a reflection of their unique situation.

Even someone unskilled in the interpretation of TAT stories would be able to tabulate the frequency of various themes. Attitude toward nature has been postulated as a significant variable affecting how people view and use the land. On the basis of the types of stories told to certain of the cards, it was possible to classify the farmers in terms of their views of man and nature. Three categories were used: "man over nature," "man in harmony with nature," and "man under nature." Where the story made no mention of the role of nature and suggested that man was in control, that he could overcome or change the situation, it was classified as "man over nature." The following excerpts illustrate this type of attitude:

> *. . . that man is probably inspecting his ground to see what he should do to it. Probably ended up tilling it to stop the dust from blowing.*
>
> *I see a real erosion problem that should be, could be easily remedied with strip cropping or stubble mulch.*
>
> *. . . He's thinking of some way he's going to control it.*

"Man in harmony with nature" was the label used for those cases in which there was some explicit mention of the need to adjust to nature, or of the importance of the role of nature. Usually this involved some combination of the need to work, along with an awareness that the work might be in vain if nature did not do her part. Some examples of "man in harmony with nature" are:

> *. . . Lot of this could be prevented, can be prevented. Not all of it. It'll take different farming practices and nature.*
>
> *. . . They decided to put it back to grass so it wouldn't blow.*
>
> *You have to try to keep this from blowing even if you're almost sure you can't when you begin. . . . Nature will take care of it if he gives a little help.*

Cases in which the solution depended on nature, where man was the hapless victim of nature, where there was resignation, or acceptance of the dominance of nature, or where there was no suggestion that man could do anything about the drought conditions depicted, were classified as "man under nature." This type of attitude is illustrated in the following excerpts:

Haven't got much to look ahead for, very black. They never will have anything unless it gets better or they move away.

. . . This old farmer is pretty disgusted and he's wondering if it would ever rain or things would get better.

. . . Well there's been a big wind. . . . He went out to his wheat field to see if there's any chance that there'd be wheat left. 'Bout the most hopeless feeling there is in the world.

He's hoping the wind would cease and the rain or moisture would fall

The percentage of farmers from each area with each of these attitudes toward nature is shown in Table 1.

Two main features of these results stand out. First, there is the proportion of farmers with each type of attitude. The stories of two-thirds of these Plainsmen expressed the attitude, "man under nature." It seems that the Great Plains environment is sufficiently stressful so that only one-third of the farmers express feelings indicating either "man over nature," or "man in harmony with nature." The second feature is that the proportion of farmers with each of these attitudes is not appreciably different from area to area, with the exception of Kiowa County, Colorado. In each case close to 70% are in the "man under nature" category, while in Kiowa County only 42% are in that group. Kiowa County, Colorado is the most extreme of all the sample areas in terms of aridity. The original sod was only plowed-up about 20 years ago, so that some of the original settlers who came at that time are still present. And in recent years there has been a considerable thinning out of farmers and amount of cropland farmed. This combination of circumstances may have resulted in a more highly selected group in terms of personality characteristics than in the other areas where most of the individuals are there because they happened to be born there.

The frequency and range of themes such as those just discussed are readily obtainable from an analysis of TAT stories. However, deeper insights are also

TABLE 1

Percentages of Farmers by Area with Various Attitudes toward Nature

	Adams	Barber	Frontier	Finney	Cimarron	Kiowa	All areas
Man over nature	12	6	20	19	15	29	17
Man in harmony with nature	18	25	7	12	8	29	17
Man under nature	70	69	73	69	77	42	66

possible. For the purposes of my dissertation, two cards were analyzed in detail, and a later study was based on the stories to an additional one (Sims & Saarinen, 1969). The two cards analyzed in detail were Murray Card 1 (Murray, 1943) and a drought scene selected for the study (see Figure 2). Murray Card 1 is a picture of a young boy contemplating a violin which rests on the table in front of him. The personality areas generally revealed by responses to this picture are concerned with how people handle the issue of achievement (Henry, 1956, p. 240). The second card (shown in Figure 2) is a picture taken for the United States Department of Agriculture entitled, "Dust Over the Dakotas." It shows a lone figure bending into the wind as dust swirls around. It represents extreme drought conditions which are the occasional experience of all Great Plains farmers. It is thus appropriate in combination with Murray Card 1, as it reveals an actual situation the farmer is likely to face and one which is likely to affect his chances of achievement.

The Schaw-Henry technique was used in interpreting the stories (Schaw & Henry, 1956). This is a technique developed for the study of nonclinical groups. From each story is abstracted the story core or dominant theme. This theme has three parts: the initial phase which sets the stage; the manipulatory stage in which the action takes place; and the resolution or outcome. The terminology used in abstracting the themes is Murray's need-press scheme (Murray, 1962). After each person's story to a particular picture has been analyzed, the themes are classified and the groups can be compared on the basis of the frequency of various themes and the kinds of actions and resolutions found within each type of story. The following is an example of how a theme is abstracted from a story.

> *This is a boy and his violin. He is looking at it and thinking he would like to become a violinist. So he picks up the violin and tries to play. His parents are pleased and encourage him in his ambition to become a violinist. So he practices regularly and follows his teacher's instructions faithfully and eventually becomes a concert violinist.*

The issue of the story can be stated as follows: a boy, desirous of becoming a violinist (need Achievement: nAch), is encouraged by his parents (fused press Nurturance Achievement; fpNurAch), and applies himself vigorously to the task of learning how to play the violin (need Work: nWk). This leads to success (Achievement: Ach) and a good outcome (GO). In abstract need-press terms the theme of the story is:

Basic Stem	Coping Mechanism	Resolution	Outcome
nAch	fpNurAch; nWk	Ach	GO

The aim is abstraction of the story's meaning, rather than analysis of the individual storyteller's psychodynamics. Since the theoretically possible range of stories is infinite, much of the idiosyncratic richness must be lost in attempting group comparisons. The principal task in utilizing a group method of analysis is to abstract to the degree which maximally preserves that which makes one story different from another, without precluding group analysis (Sims, 1964, pp. 31–35). This type of analysis reduces the clinical judgment involved, but there still remains a certain interpretive element. [Lindzey (1961) discusses some attempts to use projective tests for comparison of groups of various types.] Since the analyst's judgment is involved in every step of the process, the question of reliability of that judgment is of great importance.

The most striking feature found in stories to Card 1 is conflict. Table 2 shows the basic stems containing this element. Eighty-eight percent of the farmers see achievement as a conflicted issue. They are either pressed to achieve and do not want to, or want to achieve but encounter obstacles. Achievement for them involves an intense emotional struggle due to conflicting aims or difficulties which discourage direct goal-directed action. This is an extremely high proportion with conflicted feelings about achievement. It is greater than the corresponding proportion among federal executives recently studied by Sims (1964), and these in turn told much more conflicted stories than business executives as studied by Henry (1948, 1949). The way in which the Plainsmen handle this conflict is illustrated in Table 3.

Essentially, the Great Plains farmers do nothing to solve the conflict they themselves have set up in their stories. Almost half (44%) do absolutely nothing. Another equally large group (46%) show only passive coping mechanisms, that is, the hero may become frustrated, unhappy, disgusted, confused, worried; or he may hope, dream, wonder, or imagine, but he takes no active steps to overcome the conflict, and as a result, the conflict continues unresolved.

In each of these conflict stories there are two opposing forces. The hero, if acting logically should choose between two alternatives. Thus, in Story Type

TABLE 2

Basic Stems Containing the Element of Conflict

Story type	Basic stem	*n*	Percentage of total
1	fpAchDom c nAuto	54	61
2	nAch c pObs	24	27
		78	88

TABLE 3
Coping Mechanisms to Card 1 Story Types with Element of Conflict

Coping mechanism	Story Type 1		Story Type 2		Total	
	n	%	*n*	%	*n*	%
Active	3	6	5	21	8	10
Passive	26	48	10	42	36	46
None	25	46	9	37	34	44
	54	100	24	100	78	100

1 the hero could either give in to the press to achieve and achieve, or not give in to it and not achieve, but maintain his autonomy. In Story Type 2, he could overcome the obstacle and achieve, or fail to do so. But as Table 4 reveals, less than one-third of these stories are resolved with either achievement or autonomy. By far the largest number leaves the issue unresolved (46%). Another 25% do not squarely face the issue. Instead they resolve it by Deference–Compliance. In these cases the heroes comply by giving in to the press to achieve, but inwardly they rebel so that the resolution is unsatisfactory. In stories without conflict a higher proportion of resolutions might be expected. But this is not the case. Even in Story Type 3, where the starting situation is without conflict, only 1 in 10 of the stories has a resolution, a further indication that achievement is indeed an unresolved issue for wheat farmers on the Great Plains.

TABLE 4
Resolutions to Card 1 Story Types with Respect of Conflict

Resolution	Story Type 1		Story Type 2		Total	
	n	%	*n*	%	*n*	%
Defc/AutoAfft	19	35	–	–	19	25
Auto	8	15	–	–	8	10
Ach	6	11	8	33	14	18
rej Ach	–	–	1	4	1	1
None	21	39	15	63	36	46
	54	100	24	100	78	100

Comparison of the outcomes for the conflicted and unconflicted stories is quite revealing (see Table 5). The outstanding fact, regardless of story type chosen, is the high proportion of stories ending with no outcome. This suggests that for Great Plains farmers achievement is an ongoing problem, for which no easy solution is seen. Contrasting the stories containing conflict

TABLE 5
Outcomes to Card 1 Story Types

Outcome	Story Type 1		Story Type 2		Totals (1 and 2)		Story Type 3	
	n	%	*n*	%	*n*	%	*n*	%
Good	17	31	8	33	25	32	1	10
Bad	16	30	1	4	17	22	–	–
None	21	39	15	63	36	46	9	90
	54	100	24	100	78	100	10	100

with those without is interesting, for it shows that those who see achievement as a conflicted issue have a higher expectation of a good outcome than those who do not. At least there is more realism in their approach to achievement, as shown in the expressed awareness of the difficulties without conflict.

The great intellectual confusion and emotional disturbance found among the stories of Great Plains farmers about achievement could be a reflection of the conditions of risk and uncertainty under which they live. They generally state the initial conditions as conflicted, then either provide no coping mechanism or adopt an essentially passive attitude. Inwardly they may be extremely agitated emotionally and use such strong terms as "frustrated," "disgusted," or "plumb aggravated" to express their feelings. But there is no simple way to solve the conflict, except by leaving. They can work, use the best farming practices, prevent extreme wind erosion; once they have done this, however, they still must wait for the rains to come. The lack of a clear solution leads to intellectual confusion, which is seen in the common use of such phrases as, "he didn't know what to do about it"; ". . . something's wrong. He acts like he's got troubles of some kind"; "he's thinking and wondering how in the world he got to be there and why."

This tentative interpretation made, it is time to look at the stories to Card B (see Figure 2) which places the farmers in an actual situation of achievement much like the ones they often face in the course of their work. How do the farmers' stories handle such a situation? What sorts of solutions do they provide? Card B (see Figure 2), with its picture of a lone figure out in the dust and wind, depicts conditions which are only too familiar to most Great Plains wheat farmers. This is reflected in the uniformity with which they describe the starting situation or basic stem. Over 90% of the stories begin with what has been coded as press Environmental Deprivation (pEDepr). The farmers recognize that the scene results from a long-term lack of moisture, which poses a serious problem for the lone figure out in the wind. They generally assess the starting situation very realistically, as is illustrated by the following excerpts, with their strong flavor of pronounced environmental deprivation:

> *There's no question about this blowing dust. Drought conditions unquestionably. . . .*
>
> *Well you have right there another example of a fellow trying to make it on this drought-parched area that he got as a farmer.*
>
> *That's another dust storm scene. Farmer observing loss of crops due to wind erosion, dry weather.*
>
> *Oh this guy there was walking out across his land. Things are looking pretty tough. Dirt is blowing.*

It seems likely that the way in which achievement is handled in Card 1 is more truly reflective of the psychodynamics of these men than Card B's stories. The former provides a relatively unstructured achievement situation; whereas the latter presents the farmer with familiar circumstances which affect his level of achievement, and for which he is better able to give a consciously structured response. Yet even with Card B, where there is a concrete case for which the farmers have had sufficient time and experience to work out regular coping mechanisms, less than half were clearly active. And these active coping mechanisms often had an unthinking, repetitive quality to them.

The foregoing discussion suggests that Great Plains farmers are most likely to handle the issue of achievement conflict in a passive manner, or to do nothing. They may become unhappy, disgusted, or upset by the press or need to achieve, but they do not rationally direct themselves toward solving the conflict which is aroused. Instead, their solution involves holding on, sticking it out, or staying with it, in the hope or expectation that eventually things will change, with time, for the better. But the large number of stories ending with no outcome, as seen in Table 6, shows that there is much uncertainty about the future, in spite of the tendency to rely on it for

TABLE 6

Comparison of Outcomes to Card 1 and Card B

	Card 1 %	Card B %
Good outcome	26	25
Bad outcome	23	16
No outcome	51	59

improvements in moisture conditions. Further evidence that both stories are about achievement is provided by the comparison of outcomes. For even though Card B presents the farmers with a familiar situation and conscious control over their stories of achievement, the results are virtually identical to those of Card 1. In addition, the basic stems are similar, for press Environmental Deprivation (pEDepr) could be recoded as press Environmental Deprivation in conflict with need Achievement (pEDepr c nAch). In both cases (Card 1 and Card B) achievement is a conflicted issue; in both cases the farmers do not know how to handle the conflict; and in both cases the conflict is essentially unresolved. The Plainsmen take a very determined stance in the face of the drought hazard; but emotional involvement with the situation and pride in the ability to endure the very real distress due to drought conditions far outmeasure the ability to seek out solutions or logical, alternative courses of action.

Some obvious implications for future government policy stem from this analysis. First of all, any idea of resettling Great Plains farmers elsewhere is unlikely to meet with much enthusiasm in the area, since the farmers so rarely consider such an alternative, and since they take such pride in "sticking it out." Nor, for the latter reason, whould voluntary diminishing of the numbers of farmers currently there be expected.

A second implication is that new methods may not be readily accepted by large numbers of the farmers because they see success as the ability to hold on until the rains return. Many expressed the sentiment that there is nothing you can do when it gets dry and it does not matter much what you do when there is enough moisture.

This second implication seems to be at odds with the opinions of various Great Plains observers who speak of those in the drier areas as "heads-up farmers," and among the most innovative they have observed. It also fails to fit the facts of the very rapid adoption of stubble mulch since the drought of the 1950s. But one should bear in mind that the technique utilized is one of group interpretation. In studies of diffusion of innovations in rural areas, the proportion of innovators has always been small in relation to total numbers: heros are few and far between in any field of endeavor. One of the limitations of group analysis is the masking of wide individual differences to provide a group generalization. In stating that most Great Plains wheat farmers are not actively seeking solutions, one is not saying they are less active in this regard than other groups of farmers: it may be that they are more so. But the writer knows of no studies of other groups of farmers with which a direct comparison is possible. Knowing that the majority of Great Plains wheat farmers are not actively seeking direct solutions to the drought problem can in itself be useful for a person trying to introduce new practices into the area. Rather than trying to convince all farmers, he could more fruitfully channel his energies toward certain of the more innovative types through whom the ideas could eventually diffuse to the others.

The next two examples of the application of projected techniques in geographic research are essentially similar in that in both cases the subjects are asked to sketch a map. However the areas to be sketched differ in scale. The first is the University of Arizona campus which has usually been seen and is small enough to be intimately known by each subject. The second area is the world. No one will have seen all of it, and the world map can be understood only as a concept.

In several classes over the past few years, I have used a modified version of a technique developed by Kevin Lynch (1960) to try to determine the image of the campus held by University of Arizona students (Saarinen, 1967). In the fall of 1967 the most comprehensive study of this sort was completed. A total of 200 students from 12 different departments participated. Each student was given a blank sheet of paper and asked to sketch on it a map of the "university area" (see Figure 3). The term university area was used deliberately to see whether the students would include on their map any nearby portions of the city which they considered to be related to the campus. The main idea behind this exercise is that by examining the types of things included or omitted, one can obtain a good idea about what aspects of the environment stand out in the individual or group image of the campus, and which aspects are passed over or forgotten.

Among the most striking results are the wide range in individual differences in images and the surprisingly parochial view of many people. Maps vary in degree of detail and number of features included: some approach official charts of the campus in completeness of coverage and accuracy of detail; but most people do not recall all features, and their maps do not include many buildings, paths, or even broad areas. In some cases only a small portion of the campus is included, usually the area most frequented by the student or most central on the campus. In extreme cases only a few features are remembered and related to each other.

When features on individual maps were tallied and totals determined for separate classes, interesting patterns became apparent. Students from each department tended to introduce greater accuracy in areas where most of their classes might be expected to take place. A clear example was provided by the Women's Physical Education Department. Almost all students included their own building and most of the major buildings on the east end of the 3rd Street Mall. The result for them was, in general, a much more elongated campus image than that of most groups, whose images tended to fade out a bit along the eastern edge. As one might have suspected, the gym and stadium also stood out strongly on the maps of the women in physical education.

Because of group differences in the frequency with which various features were noted, an attempt was made to select a sample which contained students from a wide range of campus locations. It was expected that a composite campus image could be determined by combining the maps of groups with different daily ranges and centers of activity. The composite campus image should reveal which features, areas, or paths provided the most salient images. By implication one might gain some ideas for strengthening the campus image through providing the types or arrangements of features which led to an environment to which people can relate in a meaningful manner.

The composite campus image which resulted can best be explained in terms of three factors: location, function, and design. These factors interact, rather than work in isolation, but it is clear that each is important. To provide the framework for consideration of these factors, discussion will first focus on the full extent of territory included within the student image (see Figure 4).

The edges of the university area the the paths within it vary in clearness; but, in general, the extent of the maps coincided with the area of the campus proper. Only occasionally were fraternity and sorority houses or any businesses on the edge of the campus included.

The eastern and western edges stand out clearly, while to the north and south the campus tends to fade out gradually from the center. The strongest edge is on the west where a major street (Park Avenue), a stone boundary wall, and a small commercial district are found. No clear boundary was apparent in either the north or the south. Often the maps trailed off in these directions, with no firm boundary.

The location near pathways and crossroads is a major factor determining whether a feature is included or omitted on a map. Old Main in the most central location at the crossroads of the major traffic routes was the landmark most mentioned. All the buildings along the Central Mall stand out more sharply than those on lesser traveled pathways. There is a clear tendency for the campus image to fade out around the edges, especially in the south and north where there is less pedestrian traffic.

The function of a building is also of great importance in determining whether it is remembered and noted. After Old Main, the two most frequently mentioned buildings were the Student Union and the Main Library. These, of course, are used almost on a daily basis by most students throughout their university career regardless of departmental affiliation. Following the above mentioned buildings, in frequency of inclusion are: the Admini-

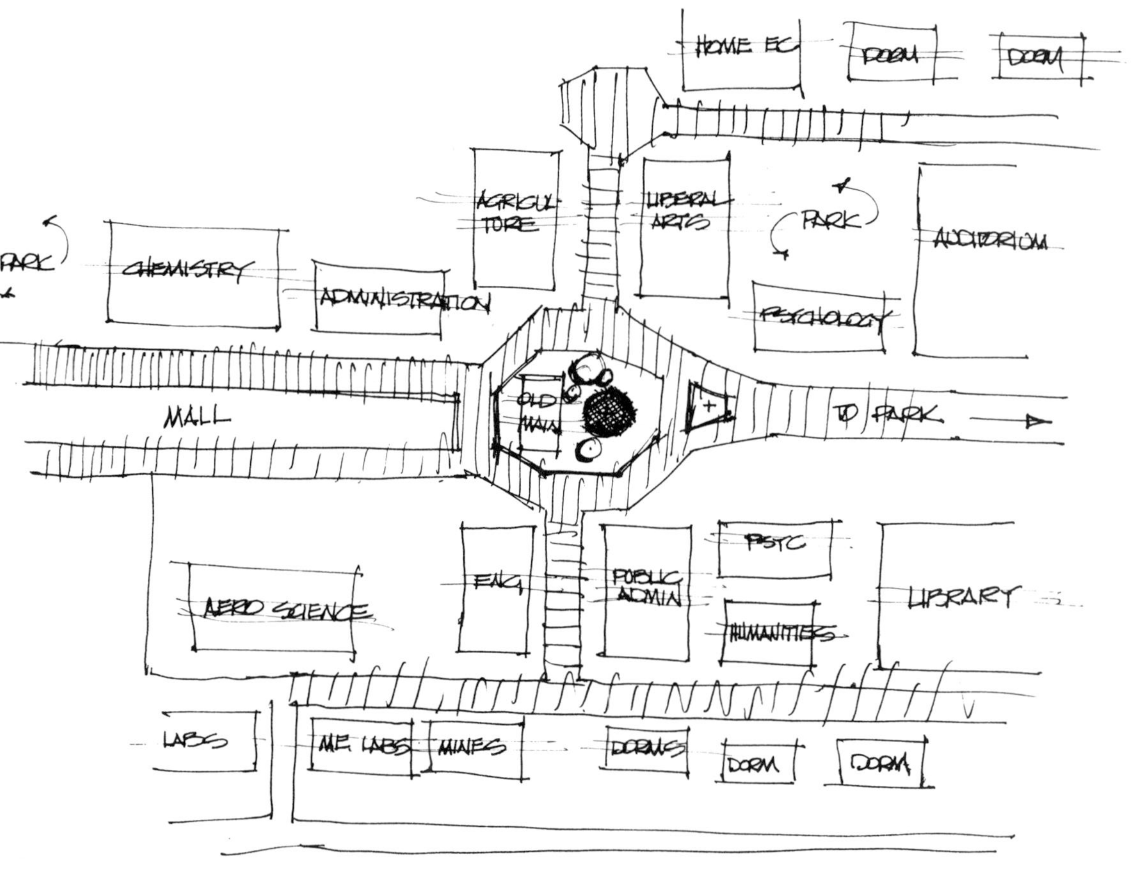

Fig. 3. *Student's map, University of Arizona campus.*

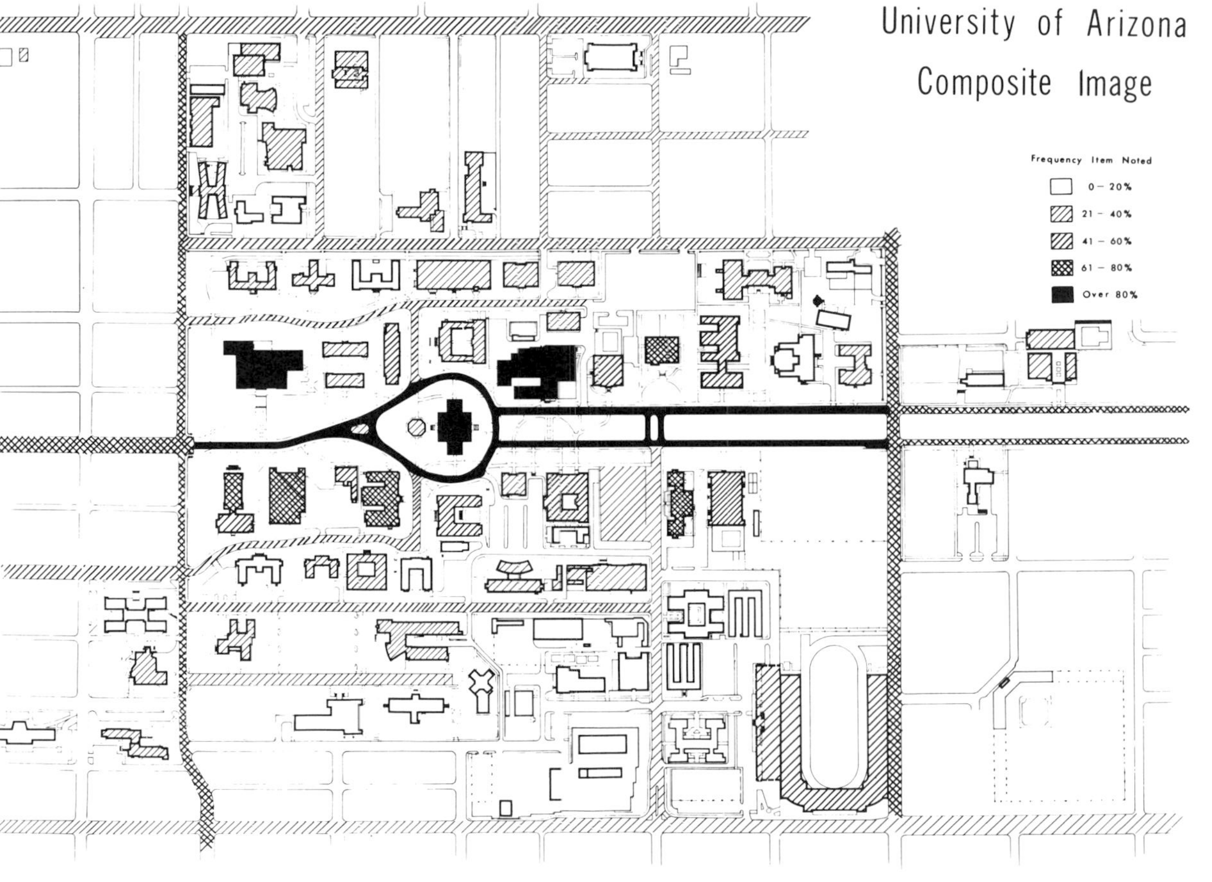

Fig. 4. *Composite map, University of Arizona campus.*

stration Building, the Science Library, and the Auditorium. All are frequently used by every student, which might help explain their prominence.

The design or arrangement of groups of buildings also helps to explain the saliency of their image. Old Main's prominence in all maps can be explained in part by its place in the arrangement of campus buildings. It is centrally located and clearly visible from more directions on campus than any other structure. It forms a part of the central design unit around the Mall. Other buildings around the main mall west of Old Main stand out very strongly as a group. However on the opposite side of Old Main, where the buildings do not form as clear a design group because of a lack of closure to the east, they do not stand out as clearly.

Some implications for future campus planning may be derived from a consideration of the composite campus image. A more clearly defined area would result if strong edges could be provided. This is especially evident in the north and south where new buildings are extending outward in a seemingly haphazard way, with no clear boundary to contain them. But strong edges are not enough. More concern for creation of well-designed groups of buildings is necessary to produce a coherent campus image. With few exceptions, such groupings are not found in the newer portions of the campus; and it is suggested that this is one of the main reasons that the image of the campus becomes vague as one moves outward from the older areas.

The final study I would like to note briefly concerns student views of the world (Saarinen, 1971). Four groups of high school students in the United States, Canada, Finland, and Sierra Leone were issued a blank sheet of paper and asked to sketch a map of the world, labeling all places they considered interesting or important. Analysis of these data should indicate which regions or countries are most included or omitted. One might expect distinctive ethnocentric views of the world to emerge for each group.

Immediately apparent in the most cursory examination of student sketch maps of the world is the predominance of the nation or country as the most frequent type of feature. On the world scale, this seems to be the most convenient size of building block, corresponding to states or provinces on the scale of a nation, or blocks within cities. Over half of the names placed on the maps were those of countries. Minor political units, mainly consisting of states or provinces within the larger countries, are often as great in size as many nations. This is true of the Canadian provinces and the states within the United States. These make up almost another 10% of the total features. Continents are almost too large to be labeled, except in cases where the students appear ignorant of smaller-sized features. The best sketch maps generally did not include the names of continents and oceans, while the poorest ones contained little else. While the cruder maps labeled only oceans, the better ones often omitted them, but tended to note the names of smaller seas, gulfs, and straits. The only features of relatively small size frequently included were cities, indicating that the students perceive the importance of cities. It also emphasizes another factor common to almost all maps, the predominance of human over physical features. Rivers, mountains, deserts, and lakes are included only occasionally.

For a broad overview the reader is referred to Table 7 which shows the number and percentage of map references devoted to each continent by each sample group. A definite home continent bias is always present despite great differences in the number of features noted by each group. This illustrates the factor of proximity, that is, the areas close to home are better known than those farther away.

For each of the sample areas, a composite political map was constructed based on the percentage of the sample which included some mention of each nation. The maps of the Finnish students indicated clearly some of the features common to the North American students as well. Also noted are some factors which explain the results. On the very broadest level one could generalize that the largest and the most highly developed nations are most familiar, while the smaller and economically underdeveloped nations tend to be less well known. North America, Europe, and Australia appeared on most maps of these students: Africa, Asia, and, to some degree, South America had more blank spaces and distortions of size and shape. In other words, the students from Finland, Canada, and the United States seem to be most familiar with the countries which are closest to them in most characteristics. Nations widely divergent in character cannot generally be identified unless they are extremely large, distinctive in shape, or have been in the news recently.

The world's giant countries, those of continental dimensions, the U.S.S.R., the United States, Canada, Australia, Brazil, China, and India were almost always included. Greenland also was generally well known, perhaps in part because the most popular school map projection, the Mercator, tends to exaggerate its size.

Some nations of smaller size appeared with great frequency because their distinctive shapes make them easy to recall; Italy, with its striking boot shape, is the prime example. No doubt Italy is remembered as a boot–in one humorous case even toes were included (see Figure 6). Another good example is Chile, which is the second most mentioned South American country: although several others are larger in area and population, the shoe string shape of Chile makes this country more memorable.

TABLE 7

Number and Percentage of Map References Devoted to Each Continent

Continent[a]	Country and map maker									
	Sierra Leone		U.S.A.		Canada		Finland		Total	
	n	%	*n*	%	*n*	%	*n*	%	*n*	%
Asia	42	14.1	357	18.1	375	11.8	640	17.6	1414	15.6
Europe	40	13.4	504	25.6	873	27.5	1609	44.2	3026	33.3
Africa	72	24.2	136	6.9	271	8.5	358	9.8	837	9.2
North America	45	15.1	575	29.2	1010	31.8	553	15.2	2183	24.0
South America	24	8.0	162	8.2	301	9.5	248	6.8	735	8.1
Oceania	24	8.0	74	3.8	144	4.5	98	2.7	340	3.7
Antartica	4	1.3	21	1.1	20	.6	15	.4	60	.7
Others[b]	47	15.8	141	7.2	179	5.6	123	3.4	490	5.4
Total	298		1970		3173		3644		9085	
Percentage		9.9		24.6		42.3		45.6		34.3

[a]Ranked according to population.
[b]Includes oceans, seas, and straits which cannot clearly be placed within a continent, plus the island of Greenland.

The effect of current events is noted in the great arc around the southern rim of Asia, from Turkey to Indonesia. This entire area was poorly represented on student maps. Only India, in the center; the distinctive peninsulas of Turkey and Saudi Arabia on the south and west flanks; and the countries currently in the news, Israel, Vietnam, Laos, Cambodia stood out in an otherwise unfamiliar area. Egypt, Nigeria, and the Congo, also much in the news in recent years, were among the few African countries noted with any regularity. In terms of student knowledge as displayed in sketch maps of the world, Africa is still the Dark Continent.

So far discussion has centered on factors common to all groups which help to explain the results. Some of those noted are the factors of size, shape, current events, and culture. In addition, there are several factors which lead to regionally distinctive views of the world. One such factor is the tendency to be most familiar with places closest to home. The following discussion, based on individual maps, provides some examples of proximity.

The same set of factors which operated to produce the New Yorker's Map of the United States is found on the world scale (1936). An extreme case is Figure 5. Here the Finnish student placed an exaggerated Finland at the center of the map. The continent of Europe covered a major portion of the globe with somewhat shrunken versions of other continents around the edges. Some extreme distortions of shape and distance occurred. Finland was larger than Canada and the length of the Baltic Sea was double the distance from Ireland to North America.

A frequent feature of maps by North American students was the placement of North and South America at the center. This has the unfortunate consequence of splitting Asia into two portions which trail off on either side of the map so that a clear image of its size and shape is difficult to obtain. As in the Finnish map, the greatest detail is found in places closest to home. A curious example of this sort was provided by a map drawn by a student from Tucson, Arizona. Here the closest foreign country, Mexico, just 60 miles away, was seen as larger than Brazil. Such exaggerations of the size of Mexico are a common feature of Tucson students. The tendency to increase the size of familiar areas and diminish the size of those unknown is illustrated as well. Africa, with only one specific place name, was drawn as a tiny continent smaller than either South America or Europe, and dwarfed by comparison with North America. A vast, vague Asia was apparently also unfamiliar. The labels indicate that the student realizes many large countries are in that continent, though he has difficulty arranging them correctly. A contrast to these maps by North Americans was provided by a sample from Sierra Leone: an accurately rendered Africa was clearly the most important continent in

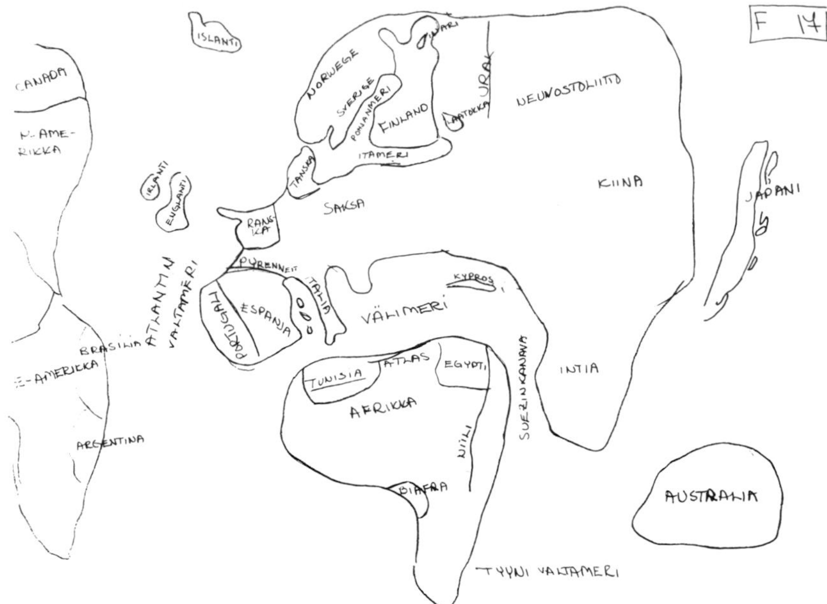

Fig. 5. *Finnish student's world map.*

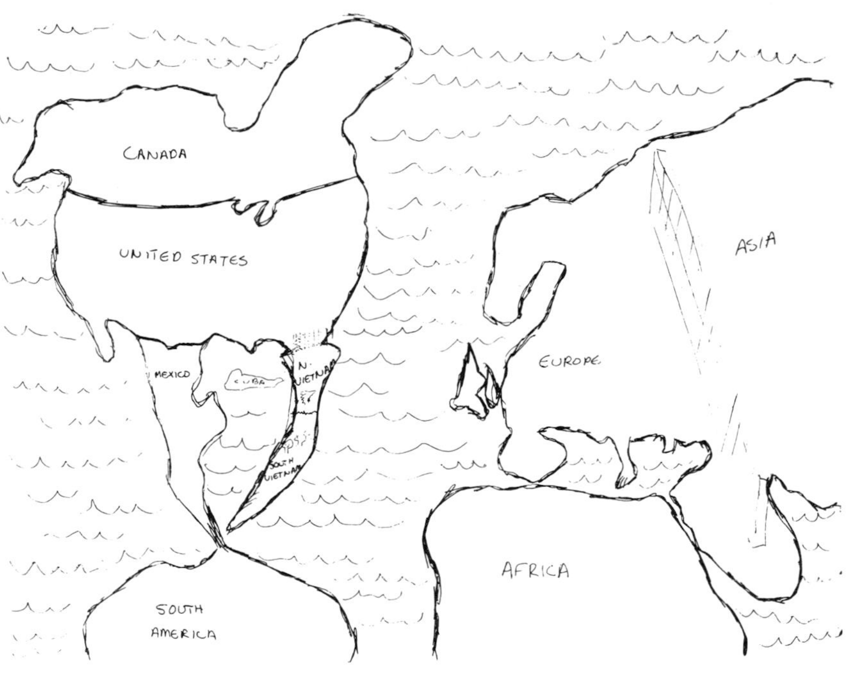

Fig. 6. *Map by "Richard Nixon, a boy, 17 years old."*

terms of position, while all other continents suffered great distortions of shape. But of all the maps, the one with which the author has taken the greatest liberties is Figure 6. It was signed, in shaky script, "Richard Nixon, a boy, 17 years old." Although humorous in intent, it underlined a feature of many of the American maps, in which an awareness of certain South East Asian countries looms large. In this case the boy brought the war home, for Vietnam is attached to the United States in place of Florida.

Analysis of sketch maps of the world indicates that definite ethnocentric images do appear, along with a number of common features. Greater contrasts may have been obtained if the sample were more carefully selected along such dimensions as developed–undeveloped or communist–capitalist, dimensions found to be important by Robinson and Hefner (1968). An analysis of voting patterns in the United Nations by Russett (1969) revealed six different coalition groups which he labeled the Western Community, Brazzaville Africans, Afro-Asians, Communist Bloc, Conservative Arabs, and Iberia. This is a more complex and subtle view of world political groupings, than is generally found. To what degree would such groups share a common image of the world, and in what ways would they differ? Analysis of sketch maps of the world could help to answer such questions which are of great importance if Boulding (1959) is correct in his assertion that to avert dangers in our unstable international system, more sophisticated world images are required.

Several conclusions can be derived from the above discussion. First there is an increasing application of projective techniques of all types in geography. A good reason for this is their utility in tapping the subjective world, something difficult to do as well by other means. Projective techniques also have the advantage of being useful for cross-cultural work, since such things as pictures and maps can transcend language barriers. A problem, however, is involved in interpretation. This is especially true in cases involving interpretation of individual psychodynamics, making it unlikely that geographers, by themselves, will attempt many studies like that using the TAT among Great Plains farmers.

The second main point of this chapter is that a collaboration between psychologists and geographers might be especially fruitful in the applications of such techniques. The psychologist's skills in projective tests applied to geographic problems could result in deeper insights into man's use of the earth. Today psychologists and geographers alike are doing research on what is here referred to as environmental psychology. But the problems attacked are different. Psychologists have been most active on the scale of personal space, room geography, and architectural space. This contrasts strikingly with most of the studies by geographers noted in this chapter, which are on the scale of the city, large regions, the nation, and the world. Another difference is the method of sampling: because the geographer is trying to measure spatial variation in environmental ideas, he selects samples from a series of different places, which is rarely considered by psychologists, who may instead select samples along psychological dimensions overlooked by geographers. Thus more collaboration between geographers and psychologists could produce most interesting and practical results.

Chapter iii

Introduction

GARY WINKEL
ENVIRONMENTAL PSYCHOLOGY PROGRAM
GRADUATE CENTER
CITY UNIVERSITY OF NEW YORK

The litany of urban problems has become so familiar that is is almost as painful to confront them in print as it is to experience them directly. A number of remedial programs has been proposed and in some cases implemented by various governmental agencies. Yet the cities do not appear to be any better. A partial explanation for this failure can be found in the assumptions which guide urban policy. Two of these assumptions are contradictory, yet both of them can be implicated in program malfunctioning.

The first assumption is that a single program can achieve a variety of different results even in areas where it is difficult to make a connection between program and outcome. Urban renewal serves as the best example of this assumption. Renewal activities were expected to provide replacement housing in deteriorating "slums," arrest the trend of urban blight, improve the city's tax base, and perhaps serve to stimulate the flagging interest of urban residents in the future of the city. Evidence which has accumulated over the past 20 years suggests that none of these outcomes has been achieved. This is not too surprising when one realizes the tenacity with which some planners and policy makers hold to the notion that the physical environment will determine behavior in a wide variety of settings. Failure to recognize the complicated interconnections which exist between human behavior and the physical environment can easily be implicated in the failure of many urban renewal ventures.

A second assumption which is equally as devastating is that which posits a direct connection between a program and its outcome. The history of job training efforts illustrates the nature of this error. If unemployment is the result of inadequate or nonexistent skills, job training is supposed to result in reduced numbers of those who are unemployed or marginally employed. Experience with these programs, however, has indicated that those who have undergone the training experience are often unable to secure jobs either because of the inaccessibility of the work place, or the exclusionary practices of labor unions. The net result is that unemployment levels remain relatively the same. Failure to consider a broad range of requirements appropriate to a specific behavior is thus likely to result in program failure.

Both of these illustrations indicate that it is necessary to begin rethinking our conceptions of the nature of urban processes. The work of urban geographers represents an important step in this direction. In the past, attention has been focused on the developmental aspects of urban physical form, the nature of the social, economic, and political linkages characteristic of differing physical forms, and those factors which account for human movement across geographical surfaces. The research which Golledge and Zannaras report in Chapter III constitutes a selection of the issues which are typically treated by those interested in the behavioral aspects of urban geography. My task will be to suggest ways in which this may be expanded.

Historically, one of the major research focuses in geography has been the understanding of those factors which account for the location of physical facilities of interest to consumers or sellers of goods and services. This issue is part of a larger question concerning the way in which geographical surfaces become differentiated through human activity. Recent research has concentrated more heavily upon the psychological processes relevant to locational decisions, since at certain scales the original formulations of the central place theorists are not adequate. This work has demonstrated that there is a relatively recurrent set of factors which account for the majority of the variance in consumer behavior. Thus, it should come as no surprise to hear that the selection of a shopping center is affected by variables such as the distance which must be traveled to the center, the range of available goods and services, the quality of the products, ease of parking, quality of service, and so on.

This research on patterns of consumer spatial behavior is important because the economic and social well-being of a number of people depend upon an understanding of the most rational allocation and location of resources. Such understanding, however, is partially dependent upon a more detailed knowledge of how various populations make use of existing resources. The work reported by Golledge and Zannaras could be fruitfully expanded to include patterns of consumer behavior characteristic of different socioeconomic and ethnic groups.

I would anticipate that the order of the variables which account for consumer behavior could very well change if comparisons were made between white middle class suburbanites and black ghetto residents. If the types and characteristics of consumer outlets varied for different populations, the planning implications could be rather interesting. One could easily anticipate the possibility that policy statements related to physical alterations in the city would be required to include a finer grained analysis of the range of spaces, goods, and services required for those groups affected by the physical changes.

If it turned out that research on patterns of consumer behavior demonstrated that the current options available to different socioeconomic groups were not satisfactory, then it might be necessary to expand the range of options available to these groups. The most obvious way to accomplish this might involve increasing the awareness of, and accessibility to, existing opportunities. That this step might be essential is evident from the work of those who have investigated the cognitive maps of various socioeconomic groups. Orleans (1967) showed that residents of a black ghetto have a very restricted view of the options available to them. No doubt a significant factor accounting for this lack of knowledge is the wide pattern of overt and subtle discrimination practiced against black people. But equally important is the availability of the means whereby people actually have access to goods and services. If the transportation system is poor, the possibilities for the expansion of urban awareness are correspondingly restricted. As a consequence, simple formulations based on variables typically employed by locational analysts would fail to account for the diversity of consumer behavior characteristic of a heterogeneous urban population.

The issue of expanding awareness of a city also raises some further questions about the work described here. In this chapter, Golledge and Zannaras report that one of the tasks which newly arrived migrants to a Midwestern city were asked to perform was the maintenance of a log of their shopping activities over time. The study accomplished its objective by demonstrating how consumer behavior changed over time until it reached a steady state. But one wonders what these new arrivals to the city learned *in addition to* the best places to shop. It is difficult to believe that perception becomes so localized that an urban traveler learns only those cues which will best guide future shopping trips. Since the city is a complex set of physical forms and behavioral patterns, the opportunities for a variety of responses are present. It is difficult to believe that people are totally oblivious to them. It would be very helpful if future research involved an expansion of the type of data reported in the consumer logs. Expanded data could include knowledge of areas of human activity, places of historical, social, or governmental significance, potential recreation areas, and so on. It is certainly true that the ability to conceptualize the city in a variety of modes is not essential, but it is equally true that the experience of living in a city should consist of something more than simply knowing that set of paths which lead to the nearest grocery or jewelry store. It is a question of being able to combine the various resources available in an urban setting in a way which will be most satisfying to the residents of a city.

One way to achieve this objective is implicit in another of the studies which Golledge and Zannaras report. They state that they have been trying to understand how people employ various environmental cues to assist the process of orientation. This research could be advanced by consideration of the work of urban designers who are equally concerned about making the city more legible, perceptually accessible, and diverse. The nature of their contribution will become clearer when it is considered how urban geographers have approached the problem of urban imageability.

Given the historical development of urban geography it is not surprising that Golledge and Zannaras should investigate the role of land use as an organizing factor in learning a city. Clearly there are behavior linkages which exist among different land uses. It could also be assumed that knowledge of a particular land use might lead to a set of hypotheses about related uses and thus serve as a cue to orientation. It must be remembered, however, that there is a wide range of three-dimensional objects which contribute to the form of cities–buildings, streets, sidewalks, and parks all make a contribution. Kevin Lynch (1960) and others have suggested how the design character of these elements, their locations, and positions relative to one another all contribute to the clarity of the urban image. The inclusion of such factors of specific concern to designers would be more likely to suggest which combination of physical features (land use *and* design elements) affects imageability.

If a decision is made to expand the study through the inclusion of design factors, alterations in experimental procedure are necessary. These alterations are desirable in any case since people do not view cities from the sky, as they are essentially required to do when they look at the two-dimensional land use maps which are currently employed. In addition, these representation systems are difficult for people who are not familiar with planners' maps, or have problems reading road maps, to understand. Actual experience with an environment or the use of small-scale environmental models lead to easier comprehension.

Of the two choices, however, the scale model is preferable. Aside from the logistical problems connected with transporting people to a field setting, there is the more critical issue of determining the nature of the environmental input(s) under these uncontrolled conditions. The use of a simulated environment has the advantage of allowing the introduction of controlled change into the study. Thus, it would be possible not only to allow simulated changes in land use, but also in the three-dimensional aspects of urban form mentioned earlier.

The utilization of actual models of the environment allows the possibility of a closer reenactment of the experience of learning to orient in the city. It is essential that the perceptual information available to the perceiver of the simulated environment match, as closely as possible, the information available were that person actually in the environment. This can be accomplished through the use of special lenses attached to the pick-up device (still, movie, or television camera). The technical details of such a procedure are now being worked out by Donald Appleyard and Kenneth Craik at the University of California, Berkeley. Using their device it is possible to take a simulated walk or ride through almost any type of environment.[1]

In conclusion, I think that the issues raised by the research described by Golledge and Zannaras are important to an understanding of the locational and movement activity of urban residents. At a broader level, however, one can question a very important assumption upon which such locational research rests: the requirement that actual movement is necessary. When the original theoretical work in this area was undertaken over 40 years ago, it was natural that the assumption of actual movement would not be seriously questioned. The current availability of alternative modes of communication (the telephone and television being the best examples) may make it less necessary to require an assumption about movement. The location of goods and services would then be subject to different sets of considerations than those occasioned by the requirement that the potential consumer travel to "a place." If communications alternatives to actual movement gained in popularity, one could begin to speculate on the likely design of future cities—cities which responded now to different forces. Such thinking might not only guide the future face of the city, but the character of urban geography and environmental research as well.

[1] Information regarding techniques for environment simulation was obtained from D. Appleyard and K. Craik, personal communication, 1971.

Cognitive Approaches to the Analysis of Human Spatial Behavior

REGINALD G. GOLLEDGE
GEORGIA ZANNARAS
DEPARTMENT OF GEOGRAPHY
THE OHIO STATE UNIVERSITY

For the most part, geographers have been interested in overt behavior. They have focused on the acts of people moving from point to point in space; and the fact that things in general vary from place to place in space; and in doing so create distributions and patterns which have a spatial existence and which beg explanation. For many years the fact that overt behavior was the result of a complicated decision-making process was ignored by geographers. Consequently, their dependent variables were measured in terms of quantities of movement, distances between origins and destinations, or other objective physical properties of the spatial act. The geographer's search for information pertained to things such as properties of distributions, interactions, network connections, patterns, surface properties, and hierarchical elements. His task involved identifying, classifying, regionalizing, and describing specific spatial systems or specific human activity systems. Frequently he was able to provide a meaningful answer to the question of "what is there?" Even more frequently, in his attempts to achieve an explanation of why things were as he described, he would search for physical correlates within the spatial structure in which distributions were found or in which behavioral acts took place. Thus spatial activity within any given system was explained in terms of covariations with selected physical properties of a given system or adjacent systems.

Under these circumstances the concept of spatial behavior acquired a rather vague meaning. The same term was used to describe, on the one hand, the physical manifestations of directed acts of human beings, and on the other hand, fluctuations of system elements (such as commodity flows, and urban, and regional growth). One rather prominent geographer, in fact, defined spatial behavior as "the movement of people, goods, messages, and ideas [Berry, 1968, p. 205]." This locked together spatial behaviors, which are caused, have directedness, motivation, action, and achievement, and fluctuations of nonsensate systems elements, which can be recorded only in terms of volumes, directions, and other physical or mathematical characteristics. In other words, goal-direct human behaviors were combined with, and analyzed similarly to, the actions of systems elements which are generated by forces exogeneous to the things being moved (or moving). This resulted in the indiscriminate use of the same methodologies to examine all types of spatial behaviors. There was an overwhelming desire to find regularities and generalizations which applied both to human and other forms of spatial behavior.

In geography then, two major approaches to the analysis of human spatial behavior can be identified. In one, behavior is reduced to its geometrical components of points, lines, vectors of force, and so on; and a consequent attempt is made to interpret the results in terms of physics-type analogues. By recording, measuring, and describing behavior in these terms, one can use the powerful mathematical tools contained in many different geometries and algebras. This approach can be used either when analyzing human behavior or when analyzing inanimate systems. In either case, the common denominator is the observable physical property or geometrical property of the system or movement in the system.

In the second approach, one also recognizes that overt spatial activity is a key problem to be explained by the geographer; but explanations for such activity are attempted in terms other than characteristics of the physical structure (or physics of structure) in which such activity takes place. This approach aims at being process oriented. It too is able to examine spatial properties of systems, for many of the elements of existing and past systems represent the manifestations of decision-making behavior on the landscape. Perhaps the single feature which distinguishes best between the two approaches is: that the structural approach reduces even human activity to geometrical components and extracts information related only to the geometry of its derived distributions; whereas the process-oriented approach places an emphasis on the human actors in a system, rather than on the working of the system itself or on its physical structure. The type of approach which we wish to emphasize is the process-oriented approach.

The remainder of this chapter consists of summaries of several experiments related to environmental learning and cognition, most of which were carried out at The Ohio State University, 1968–1971. Each experiment is related to an everyday activity performed by urban residents, and each reflects our attempts to operationalize concepts or test theory under actual or simulated "real world" conditions.

Learning in "Real World" Enivornments

The idea that human spatial behavior is an outcome of sequential decision-making processes and may be expected to vary over time led a number of geographers to investigate learning models in an attempt to explain variations in this spatial behavior. This excursion has been fruitful; it has clarified a number of significant concepts implicitly used in geography—concepts already tested and accepted in psychology. It has also led to the use of a variety of "new" models (i.e., "new" to the geographer). Some have been pursued and cultivated with a fair degree of success, while other have as yet shown relatively little reward in terms of solving the geographer's empirical problems.

Of the many theories and models available to the geographer, the greatest emphasis has been placed on: *(a)* stimulus–response models such as could be defined by linear operator learning models; *(b)* stimulus ranking models which lend themselves to analysis by multidimensional unfolding and multidimensional scaling methods; *(c)* concept identification models which can be readily formulated in Markov terms; and *(d)* a variety of cognitive learning models such as those suggested by Tolman, Lewin, and Kelly. Stimulus–response models and stimulus ranking models have been most widespread in consumer behavior studies and space preference studies (Briggs, 1969; Golledge & Rushton, 1970; Huff, 1962; Rushton, 1969a-c). Concept identification models and cognitive learning theories have been used primarily in urban perception problems (Golledge & Zannaras, 1970), particularly for identifying cues which help individuals locate themselves in urban areas and act as focal points for building images of the urban area.

The following section focuses on our initial uses of stimulus–response and incremental learning ideas, in an attempt to illustrate some types of experiments which have been undertaken with a specific learning theory bias.

The Journey-to-Work Game

Learning to Operate in Familiar Environments

This particular experiment was designed by J. Jakubs and S. Weiskind (in a learning theory seminar in the Department of Geography at The Ohio State University in 1968) to show that trial-and-error experimentation is undertaken on a very limited basis for some types of urban activities. We hypothesized that some form of routinized behavior develops; but, because of the exigencies of the decision-making process with respect to selecting a journey-to-work pattern, and the ability of individuals to generalize from one urban setting to another, only a limited number of experimental trials occur. We also postulated that journey-to-work patterns differ somewhat from the spatial behavior patterns developed in the process of shopping activities (or say, recreational activities), because the goals associated with the former trips are clearer in the minds of subjects (both in the experimental and in the real world). In addition, some type of time or cost minimization process is assumed to dominate in the selection of routes. Thus route selection is considered to be an avoidance process, whereby the checks to movement (such as stop signs and street lights) are minimized within the overall framework of trying to achieve some minimum time or minimum cost goal. For an activity as consistent as going to and from work, it was also hypothesized that the amount of experimentation is small because of the need to develop a pattern of behavior which minimizes the number of decisions to be made in terms of selection of route segments. While the results of the experiment are by no means conclusive, they provided some evidence for the hypotheses advanced.

The experiment was fairly simple. Subjects were graduate students in the geography department of The Ohio State University. Each subject was given a map of a road system. On the map were sketched the location of traffic lights and stop signs, and each linear segment of the transportation system had a maximum speed restriction allocated to it (see Figures 1 and 2). Unknown to the subjects, travel time had been estimated for each segment of the road. Each subject was instructed to start from point A and make a trip to point B. The subjects were told to repeat the experiment until they felt that they had established either a single route which they would prefer to follow on all successive trials, or until they had established a subset of routes which could be ordered in some hierarchical fashion. This "habit family" of routes would then be used such that the most preferred route would be chosen, except when various barriers to movement, or curiosity, or boredom, stimulated the selection of a route further down the hierarchy.

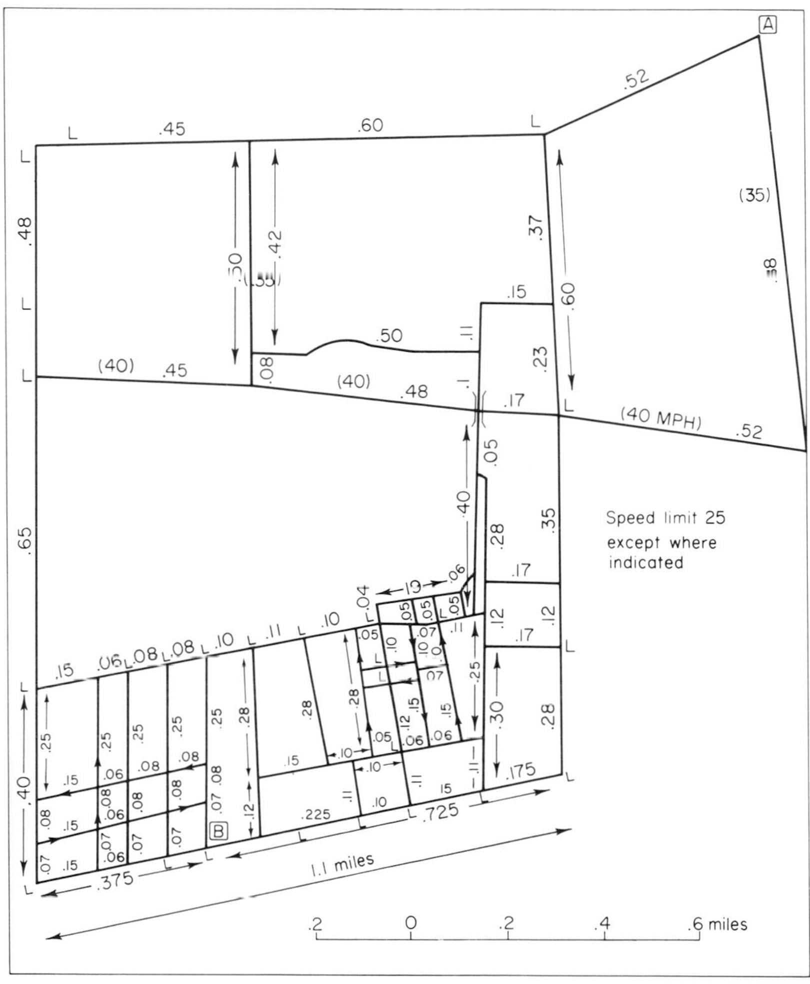

Fig. 1. *Journey-to-work: distance and barriers.*

Subjects were informed of penalties associated with each traffic light and stop sign. Two major categories of penalties were assessed. At intersections where the traffic light symbol was indicated by a double circle, the green–red phase was taken to be 90 sec. At traffic lights or stop intersections with a single circle, the green–red phase was assumed to be 30 sec. Each subject was instructed to start from point A and to develop a route to point B, using whatever combinations of line segments he wished. Any time a subject came

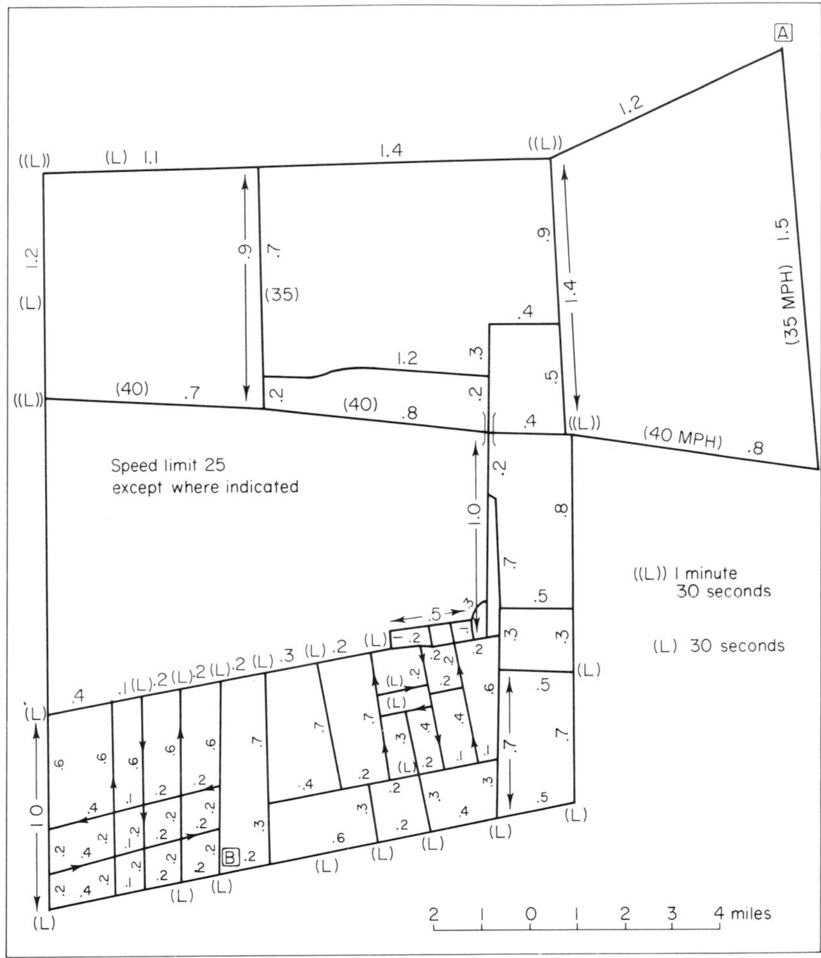

Fig. 2. *Journey-to-work: times and light phases.*

to a traffic light he threw two die. The odds were calculated such that he was given a 50–50 chance of hitting a red or green phase at each light. The first die determined whether or not he had to check his progress at a street light or stop sign. The second indicated the amount of time he would have to stop at that intersection. For the shorter stops, 5-sec gradations were determined (i.e., if the subject threw a five he had to wait 25 sec, or was penalized 25 sec, before moving away from the light). For the larger lights, each number on the die was taken to represent 15 sec.

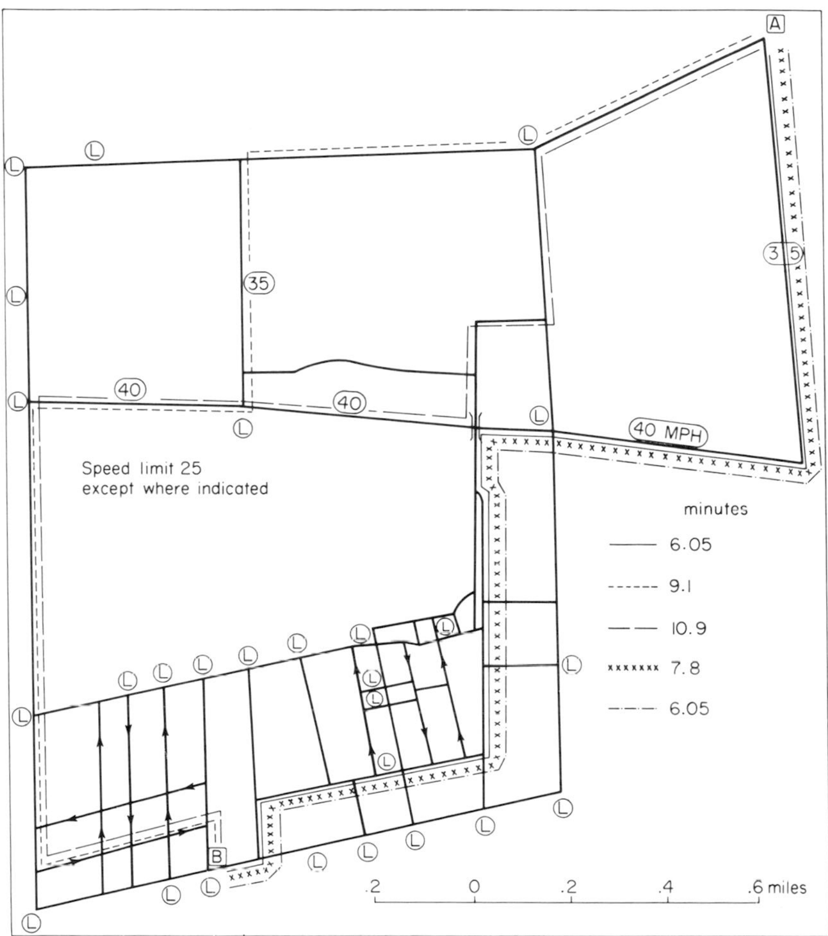

Fig. 3. *Journey-to-work: subject 1.*

As previously stated, Figure 2 shows the map as presented to the subjects, together with all the appropriate information related to the time taken to cover each segment of the road. One set of sample output is also presented (Figure 3). This subject took five trials. Although he actually chose what turned out to be a highly satisfactory route on the first trial, he still undertook some experimentation before returning to the initial route. In terms of the times taken on each experimental trial, the original trial took 6.05 min; the second, 9.1 min; the third, 10.9 min; the fourth, 7.8 min; and the fifth, 6.05 min. Note also that routes chosen on the second and third trials differed substantially from the initial trial, but that the subject very quickly discarded those trials.

Another subject undertook three trials before stating he had satisfactorily developed a pattern that he would repeat on all future trials. In the limited amount of trial-and-error exploration, he experimented with only reasonably adjacent line segments, and most feasible alternative routes were not even tested. The difference in time between the shortest and longest trials was only .9 min.

Yet another subject undertook four trials, and the differences in times over trials depended on either catching or not catching a stop light. In other words, he settled immediately on a basic travel pattern and after experimenting with variations in times along that route, considered that it was satisfactory as far as his aspirations were concerned.

One of the interesting things about this experiment was related to the experimental map itself. It was a simplified, translated, and rotated map of the Ohio State University campus and surrounding areas. The origin point was in the vicinity of a set of university apartments where most of the subjects lived. When asked before testing if he recognized the map, no subject was able to identify it. After the experiment had been conducted, the subject was again asked if the map was at all familiar, and again he replied in the negative. Each subject was then asked to draw a map of the journey-to-work pattern used on his regular visits to the university. For those who lived near point A, the maps so drawn were compared with the pattern developed after trial-and-error experimentation. In every case except one, the individuals had almost duplicated their regular work trips. Even in this one case, the regular work trip had been approximated. The subjects were never told that the abstract map on which they were working was in any way related to their actual locations, and subsequent questioning of sample members revealed that none had made this association.

Thus from this simple journey-to-work experiment, we were able to draw several conclusions. Some type of trial-and-error experimentation was frequently involved in developing a journey-to-work pattern. The amount of experimentation was small, as was the number of trials to develop suitable travel patterns. The greatest number of trials taken by any sample member was five, and most members stopped the experiment after three trials. Considering the short lengths of experimentation and the fact that most patterns were relatively invariant after three or four trials, we decided not to attempt to fit any of the standard mathematical learning models to these data. One would have to have a large learning parameter to achieve a fully learned response after such a small number of trials; and it was argued that the validity of any parameter estimated in this case would be highly suspect. However, we were satisfied that some experimentation did take place prior to the selection of journey-to-work travel patterns, and most subjects agreed that they would develop some habitual pattern for their work trips. This means that one particular phenomenon in the urban environment (i.e., the journey to work) is probably highly stable, relatively invariant, and consequently, is potentially highly predictable. This gives some support, then, to the use of simple gravity-type models to explain urban travel behavior, and the tendency to predict travel behavior with fairly simple mathematical models.

Consumer Behavior

Learning to Shop

One of the features of the journey-to-work model which made it difficult to describe in terms of any standard mathematical learning model format, was that relatively invariant behavior occurred too quickly to get reliable estimates of the rate of learning. Shopping behavior, however, is generally regarded as dynamic, with equilibrium patterns of behavior which are, at best, temporary. This is certainly so for the high-order goods (e.g., shopping goods, or goods found only in large shopping centers). For low-order goods, (i.e., goods directly related to the day-to-day subsistence of individuals, such as grocery shopping), while some variable shopping patterns are retained by individuals, there is also a tendency to develop habitual patronage patterns. One can study the market decision process by taking a neophyte shopper, placing him in an unfamiliar environment, and speculating about his behavior over a series of trials. This behavior can be described in a stimulus–response framework and can be modeled in terms of linear operator learning models or Markov chains (Golledge, 1967a, b; Golledge & Brown, 1967).

In either case, one assumes an initial search period where alternative members of some feasible opportunity set are sampled on successive trials. Relative degrees of success or failure are then recorded by the individual, in attempts to eliminate unfavorable alternatives from the behavior patterns. There is a constant feedback of information about places visited, a constant reconciliation of rewards and aspiration levels for each of the alternatives tried, and the evolution of some preferred behavior pattern. Ideally this pattern reduces to a single center choice syndrome (Berry, 1968; Christaller, 1966; Golledge, Clark, & Rushton, 1965; Lösch, 1954). Generally, however, it narrows down to a selection of two or three alternatives, with one of these being the most preferred (see Table 1). The reasons for preferring one over another are immaterial at this point, and they have been discussed extensively in geographical journals (Berry, Barnum, & Tennant, 1962; Curry, 1967; Rushton, 1969c). The development of multiple response behavior patterns allows enough variability in the marketing act to enable individual shoppers to undertake comparison shopping, and to reduce the possibility of irregular behavior brought about by curiosity or boredom. It also allows for the replacement of the less favored alternatives if systems shocks (such as new shopping alternatives) appear on the scene.

The essence of this conceptualization is that marketing behavior consists of a search phase and some type of patterned response phase. The transition from search activity to the patterning of responses is accomplished by means of a learning process; and it should be possible to define learning parameters for different types of functions.

This conceptualization is not unique to the geographer. Nicosia (1966) has described the process as one of "funneling" of consumer search activities. The funneling process was originally formulated to describe the narrowing of brand product choices by consumers over time, as a result of their cumulated information and experiences with different products. We have previously suggested that funneling activity is a necessary outcome of spatial search activity (Golledge, 1967a, b; Golledge & Brown, 1967). We also assumed that one of the aims of search activity is the reduction of the total number of possible alternatives open to any given individual, to those which have meaning and which would have a finite probability of giving rewards as a

TABLE 1

Number of Shopping Centers Visited[a]

Number of centers visited per person		Number of persons	
1	66% (1–3)	55	
2		76	= 50% (2–3)
3		74	
4		44	
5		25	
6		7	
7		3	
No data		9	

[a]Data were obtained from a survey of approximately 290 randomly sampled households in northern Columbus (Ohio) in the summer of 1968.

result of search. While it is hypothesized that the period of search or exploration will vary from function to function, we have experimented with only one type of activity for which data can be collected in a very short time span—namely, grocery marketing behavior.

A currently popular experimental approach to the funneling process is one in which a sample of consumers is asked to keep a log book, for some time period, of all movements to buy groceries. In general, patterned behavior with respect to grocery purchases can be clearly identified after about 4–6 weeks of experimentation. Assuming that the average shopper shops for grocery products several times a week, this gives 15–30 trials per person from which to calculate necessary parameters.

Not every individual, however, is located equally with respect to his opportunity set for shopping activities; thus a range of different behaviors is possible. There are several hypotheses concerning this relationship (Golledge, 1967b):

1. Individuals located nearest to members of their opportunity set are most likely to exhibit features such as a single choice syndrome.
2. Individuals least favorably situated with respect to their opportunity set are more likely to exhibit multiple response patterns.
3. Individuals located further from their opportunity set may take longer to form a patterned response because of their need to cultivate a larger perceptual horizon.

These three hypotheses and others relating to the funneling concept have been tested in a number of different environments.

One such test was conducted by D. Rogers (1970), who obtained data from a 23% sample of the incoming migrant population in Madison, Wisconsin. Each shopper was requested to keep a travel diary for approximately 6 weeks, and to record both his initial shopping behaviors in the week prior to the initiation of this study, and behaviors immediately following his establishing residence in the city. The results indicated the existence of the funneling process in search activities. Over the study period, subjects refined their shopping activities from that of searching among as many as five or six alternatives, to regular patronage of one to three places.

This finding supports some early empirical evidence (Golledge, 1967a) of the same type of refinement of marketing behavior for a sample of hog farmers in southeastern Iowa. Again the size of the initial opportunity set was found to be five or six outlets; the final patterned response was limited to one or two. Whereas the grocery shoppers refined their patronage within a period of 6 weeks, the hog farmers took a number of years. In terms of the total number of experiences with marketing and grocery purchases however, the two studies produced approximately the same number of trials.

Rogers's study also supported two hypotheses: one, about the effect of spatial location on the narrowing of alternatives in the final patterned behavior; and another (Golledge & Brown, 1967), relating to the development of temporarily stable patterns of behavior. Temporarily stable patterns develop with respect to grocery purchases, so that the immediate needs of households can be satisfied with a minimum of inconvenience. Rogers found that the early stage of the search process frequently involved continued patronage of a limited number of alternatives until more exhaustive search behavior could take place.

By splitting the 6-week period into two 3-week periods, Rogers found a statistical difference in the mean number of different stores visited between the first and second periods of market trial. Approximately 43% of his total sample decreased the spatial variability of their store patronage from the first period of market trial to the second; 38% of the sample exhibited no change between the two periods; and 18% increased the number of places visited.

Fig. 4. *Temporal trend in spatial search activity. —: Consumers with a favorable spatial relationship to supply alternatives (Group A). (- - -): Consumers with an unfavorable relationship to supply alternatives (Group B). [After Rogers (1970).]*

Another result of the Rogers study was based on stratification of his population with respect to the locations of individuals and their opportunity sets. It indicated that the group which was least favorably located with respect to its opportunity set (and was consequently expected to incur the largest transportation cost to satisfy its shopping goals), actually exhibited more spatially variable behavior in its patronage patterns than those more favorably located (see Figure 4).

The above experiments show how some of man's normal activities can be conceptualized and modeled in terms of learning theories. The production of mathematical models to describe these different types of behavior which incorporate learning parameters and have as their output regular, or patterned, behaviors has proven difficult. Up to this stage, we have been able to provide only a general conceptual framework under which studies of this type could be undertaken. We have, furthermore, examined (in a fair amount of detail) some of the subsets of the overall conceptual model. For example, the activities of space searching are being rather exhaustively analyzed within the field of geography. Some of this work is continuing in the area of consumer behavior. Much more has been undertaken with respect to another type of urban behavior—that of intraurban migration or residential site selection.

The process of residential site selection has been formulated in operational terms, and a number of alternative models have been put forward to describe it (Adams, 1969; Brown & Moore, 1970). In addition, there are a number of empirical studies in which the location of sites visited by new homeowners prior to the selection of a new residence have been mapped; information has been extracted about the directional and distance biases of these search fields. Search fields have been analyzed for different socioeconomic groups and for people at different locations within the urban area. However, each of these studies was directed at only one small part of the total conceptual model of changing spatial behavior. Each study has benefited considerably from the use of learning theory principles; and some have explicitly been able to use various types of mathematical learning models to analyze the processes being examined. More often than not the studies are isolated, with little theoretical or conceptual background (i.e., they are simple problem-solving studies). Many more of these studies, both in the area of individual consumer behavior and individual travel behaviors (such as journey-to-work in urban areas), have to be undertaken before we can be regarded as having sufficient data for the rigorous testing of spatial learning models. What is becoming apparent is that each of the empirical studies being undertaken along the lines suggested in several conceptual models indicated that space searching is part of a sequential decision process in which trial-and-error (or at least exploratory) behavior is modified on successive trials by accumulating information, such that over a period of time, variabilities of behavior are generally decreased. This decrease makes behavior itself more predictable and somewhat easier to explain. At least if we are sure that behavior is repetitive and somewhat invariant (see Table 2), we have more confidence in searching for explanations that have generalization and scope (Marble & Bowlby, 1968).

Many of the patterns existing within different environments may be temporary patterns of behavior. Unstable conditions can be quickly introduced by changes in the external physical environment, the human environment, or the environment peculiar to the individual himself. We recognize that equilibrium spatial behaviors are subject to continual changes as information about various environments is assimilated. However, while there is room for change in many of these behaviors, and while some change actually occurs, the type and rate of change is itself a recognizable phenomenon which can be accounted for in models which have multiple patronage patterns or multiple route selections as their output.

TABLE 2

Repetition and Trip Purpose: Cedar Rapids 1949[a]

Purpose	Repetition ratio[b]	Average number of stops	Average distance to repeated stops(mi)	Average minimum distance to location(mi)	Total number of establish-ments
Grocery	.92	6.49	.46	.18	153
Bank loan and financial	.86	1.78	.89	1.00	59
Gasoline[c]	.85	1.17	.93	.26	97
Supermarket	.84	3.37	.72	.70	10
Public office	.83	2.84	.83	.38	107
Tavern[c]	.80	1.05	.63	.45	63
General store	.77	4.18	.92	.36	34
Restaurant	.73	3.53	1.68	.34	98
Theater	.71	2.49	1.29	.87	7
Confectionaire	.70	1.12	.99	.50	25
Bottle club	.69	1.43	1.03	.91	54
Department store	.67	2.64	1.61	1.15	5
Variety store	.66	1.97	1.36	.62	8
Medical	.64	1.49	1.66	.76	168
Clothing	.61	2.09	1.42	1.24	17

[a]From: Marble and Bowlby, 1968, p. 69.
[b]This represents the ratio of repetitions to total trips.
[c]These are known to be underrated.

Cognitions of Urban Structure

Geographers have a number of simple and fundamental concepts concerning the physical structure of cities and the interrelationships among segments of these cities. These concepts are summarized in a number of descriptive models, and they are being incorporated more frequently into both normative and planning models. Currently there is increased interest in the behavior of individuals within urban structures, and in the way urban structures are perceived and recorded by individuals. These last two lines of research are complementary, for it is argued that behavior within the urban structure will be directly related to the way the structure is perceived. The investigation of cognitive structures of urban areas has been undertaken with the hope of finding commonly held conceptions in the general population, so that significant generalizations can be formulated. Ideally, of course, it is hoped that individuals' conceptual structures of an urban area will in some way conform to the physical models that have been derived from objectively analyzing the locations of segments of the city in space.

Research into the cognitive structure of urban areas can be subdivided into three parts. The first is characterized by micro-level studies. The aim of this approach is to find out how well people can locate specific points in urban areas (Briggs, 1971; Golledge, Briggs, & Demko, 1969; Lee, 1970). This approach is related to the second: the problem of determining what metric is used to measure distances in urban areas. It relies on a variety of scaling techniques (such as multidimensional scaling) to extract information from data sets. The first is exemplified in the attempt to define perceptually small areas of the city—generally described by the term "neighborhoods" (Saarinen, 1964; Zannaras, 1969); the second is an attempt to reconstruct a set of urban features which are observed on journeys through the urban areas (Appleyard, Lynch, & Meyer, 1964; Carr & Schissler, 1969).

The third part occurs at a macro level. Its emphasis is on attempting to reconstruct maps of urban areas from the knowledge that individuals have about those places. Most of this work has been carried out by researchers outside the field of geography. Obviously, the results of this type of research are important to the geographer. It should be quite apparent that the geographer may be completely wasting his time attempting to find some organization in the spatial arrangement of things in urban areas if the arrangement of these things has little relevance to the way people behave with respect to them.

Of the three lines of research, the most intensively investigated subset has been the macro approach. Originating with the innovative work of Kevin

Lynch in the early 1960s, this work has been supplemented by the continuing research of Appleyard, DeJonge, Carr, Craik Lee, and others. Basically, these researchers have recognized an existing relationship between city structure and the cognitive process of individuals. Environmental images are said to result from a two-way process between the observer and the environment, in which the observer selects, organizes, and gives meaning to a limited number of features in the environment. These features provide the focal points on which urban images are built. The focal points act as orientation nodes for individuals; and the accuracy with which these points and/or places are located determines the overall accuracy of the conceptual images.

It is postulated that the particular spatial form of cities facilitates and/or inhibits the development of individual cognitive maps, and consequently may facilitate and/or inhibit behavior patterns within urban areas. It is argued that individuals are ready to perceive those elements of the environment which have a high probability of occurrence in their action spaces. Furthermore, it is recognized that the images an individual has of the external world are progressively developed as he matures and as he learns more about the environment in which he has to operate.

The geographer's interest in each of these approaches relates to a hypothesis that the cognitive images of urban areas (or subsets of urban areas) are stylized in some way. The experiments which follow in this section of the paper deal with our attempt to uncover some of the features of stylized urban images. Beginning at the micro level, we attempted to determine whether there are consistent directional or distance biases in the way people store information about selected locations in the urban area. We then moved from point-oriented data to small areal units, and attempted to develop an operational method for defining perceptual neighborhoods. The last experiment dealt with our attempts to determine if the physical structure of urban areas as a whole influences the ability of people to behave in those areas.

Experiment 1

Configurations of Points. The first experiment which relates to the cognitive structure of urban areas is a micro-level experiment. We wanted to discover how well individuals are able to locate sets of points within urban areas, and to investigate, in more detail, the relationship between distances as perceived by individuals and objective, or "real world," distances. Thus, we sought to determine whether there are consistent directional or distance biases in the way that specific points in urban areas are located; and to relate these biases to certain types of urban behavior.

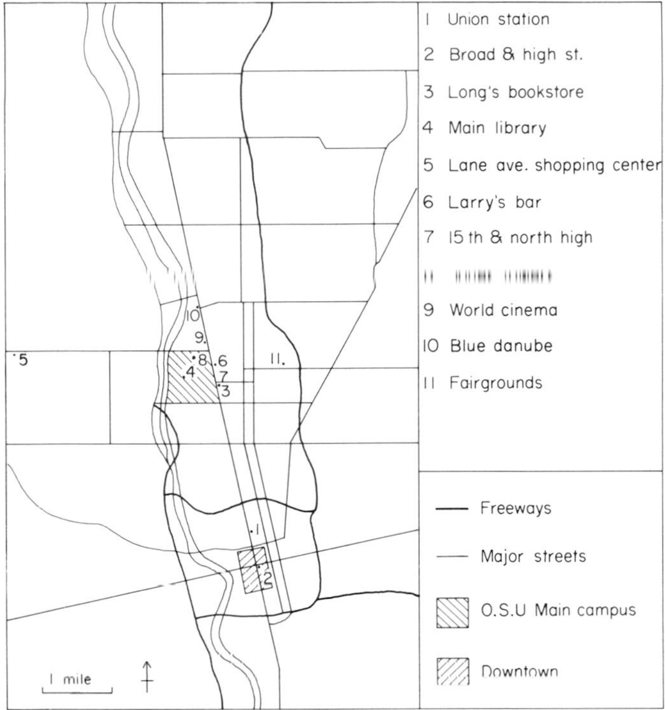

Fig. 5. *Place perception. Study area and sample points.*

The experiment was comprised of two parts which will be discussed as separate studies. The initial study was conducted in 1968: a small segment of Northern Columbus, in the vicinity of the Ohio State University campus, was selected as the study area. A limited number of well-known points were chosen with locations along a major north–south artery passing the university, in the middle suburban area, and along an artery orthogonal to the main north–south street (see Figure 5). Several points on campus were also chosen. Subjects were asked to complete two tasks: first, to estimate the closeness of pairs of points via a paired-comparison experiment; second, to estimate distances from a standard point on the campus to each of the locations. The data from the first experiment was inputted to the Kruskal IV multidimensional scaling program, in an attempt to recover a configuration of points based on the individual's conceptions of where the points lay with respect to one another. This experiment was highly successful in that the summary con-

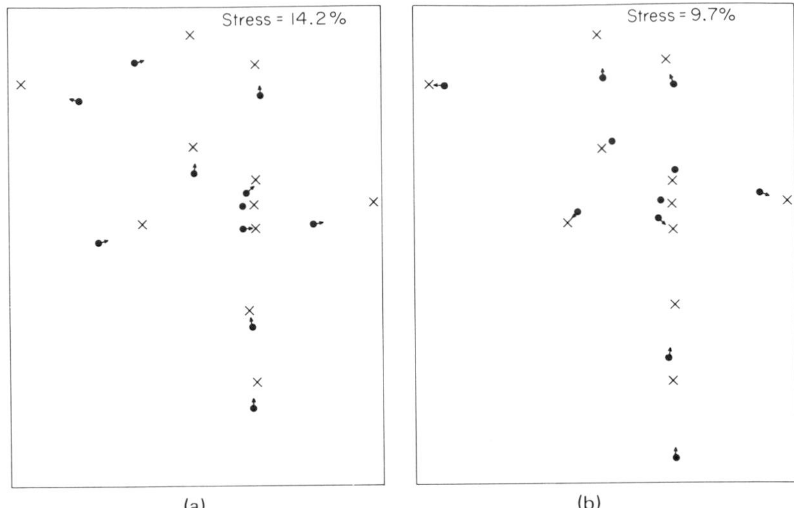

Fig. 6. *Sample subject configurations. (a) Group I; (b) Group II. (•) perceived location; (X) actual location.*

figuration obtained for the sample group closely approximated the actual configuration of points, except for some minor disturbances (see Figures 6 and 7). These disturbances showed specific biases toward, and away from, the Central Business District (CBD): along the main artery; and, as distance increased from this main artery, along the orthogonal artery.

Next the relationships between perceptual and actual distances were examined to determine whether differences existed between objective (or "real world") distances and distances as perceived by our subjects. Again a bias was noted. There was increasing disparity between perceived and actual distances in the direction of the center of the city; and underestimation of distance moving away from the downtown area. Furthermore, when the subjects were divided into two groups on the basis of length of residence in the urban area, distinct biases were noted in the degree of their overestimation and underestimation of distance (see Figure 7). The configuration of relative newcomers to an area were more imprecise than those of longer term residents. In addition, the degree of distortion for places located off the main arteries was greater for the new residents.

The differences in the two configurations and in the way that distances were overestimated or underestimated were taken as indicative of an environmental learning process which increased the subject's ability to locate points

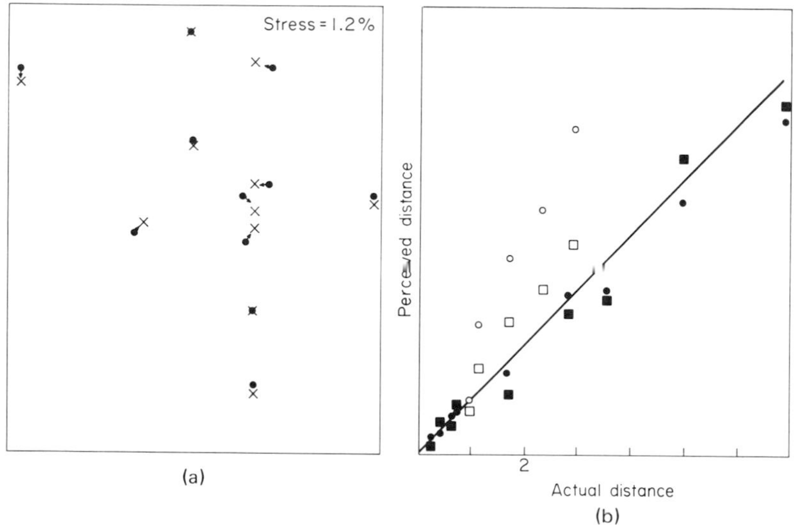

Fig. 7. *(a) Group configuration of sample points (left). The actual map is compared to the configuration derived from dissimilarity measures consisting of actual distances between points on the real map. (●) derived configuration; (X) actual configuration.*

(b) Perceived and actual distance relationships (right). Perceived distances to places along a major north-south artery passing through the campus. (□) Subject Group I, south of campus; (○) subject Group II, south of campus; (■) subject Group I, north of campus; (●) subject Group II north of campus.

within urban areas and to estimate the relative positions of points in the area, with respect to each other. It was then postulated that as more information is collected about an urban area and the location of places is learned more thoroughly, behavior changes occur. However, large-scale experimentation to prove or disprove this hypothesis has not yet been undertaken.

The second part of this experiment (Briggs, 1971) attempted to obtain a deeper understanding of the individual's cognition of spatial location, so that meaningful measures of spatial separation could be determined and subsequently incorporated into existing models relating to human behavior in urban environments.

It can be argued that the physical structure of a city, or at least those parts of the physical structure of a city which are relevant to the individual (i.e., which comprise his awareness space, or cognitive map, of the urban area), is learned over time in three ways. Information is gained directly from:

1. the city structure, using the various sense modalities
2. a symbolic representation of the city, using visual media such as maps, photographs, and written words, and from autitory media such as spoken words or broadcast message
3. inferences about parts of the city which have not been experienced through behavior or symbolic representation, but which are inferred by the process of generalizing from experiences with other spatial locations

Knowledge obtained in any of these ways appears to be spatially discontinuous. It may also be organized into some form of hierarchy, such that knowledge at a higher level is partly dependent on, and influenced by, knowledge of lower levels. Information about the physical structure might be recorded in terms of specific points, the closeness of points, spatial position and relative location, and paths linking specific sets of points. In other words, we could argue that information about city structure includes characteristics of individual attributes, proximity, directional relationships, and contiguity effects.

In a very real sense then, we are suggesting that individual spatial behavior in an urban environment is a function of the level of information one has about that environment and the way he obtains that information. In turn, the level of information collected will influence cognitions of distances, proximities, and other spatial relationships within the urban area. In this particular experiment we were not as concerned with *how* the individual obtains information from the environment, as with how his estimates of distance conform with distance estimates in the "real world"; and whether or not variations in his distance estimates are biased by selected physical features of the urban environment.

For this study, a sample of 248 students from The Ohio State University was selected. The bulk of the students lived on campus or within the immediate neighborhood of the university, and thus had similar opportunities for the development of their activity patterns. Although Briggs (1971) did not, at this stage, control for the degree of knowledge sample members had about urban environments, he did assume that they all had a minimum of similar knowledge about the immediate urban environment in which they lived. Since the university was used as a major focal point and the study concentrated on facilities in the immediate vicinity of the university, it was considered desirable to have a sample group with some potential similarity in terms of activity patterns.

For this experiment, 20 specific locations were chosen within the city of Columbus. Each location could be assigned to one of four groups: *away* from downtown, versus *toward* downtown; *along* the major north–south artery, versus *off* the artery. The main entrance to the university (approximately 2.5 miles north of downtown) served as a common origin for the points. Three criteria were used to select the locations in the city. The first was that locations in each of the four groups mentioned above should generate distances to the common focal point which were relatively similar for each group. The second was that locations chosen should be clearly familiar to the subjects. Any subject who was not familiar with any given location did not complete that part of the experiment. Third, to achieve some type of control with respect to the response of individuals, all locations were limited to the same type of node. Major road intersections were chosen as the type of location which would meet each of the above criteria.

Measures of each subject's cognition of the distance from the common origin point to each of the 20 locations were obtained in two ways. First, every subject was given 20 line scales and was instructed to place a mark on each scale representing road distance by the most direct driving route, from the common origin point to the corresponding location. The line scales were 50 cm in length and were divided in 1-mile increments up to 7 miles. Second, each subject was given a standardized length of line and was asked to represent, on another line, the road distance to a given location relative to the standard distance.

In the second case, data were collected in ratio form by dividing the length of the standard line by the length of the line marked by the subjects. These ratios were assumed to represent estimates of the ratio of road distance from the common origin point to the corresponding location. To overcome some of the pair-order effects, but to negate the problem of having each subject do 390 presentations (i.e., if each location in turn were selected as a standard point), each subject was given only 7 location pairs as standards. Each location was used as a standard by one-third of the sample group, giving a minimum of 80 sample sheets for each of the 20 locations; 133 estimates were thus requested of each subject. Remembering that subjects were instructed to avoid making distance estimates between locations with which they were unfamiliar, the actual number of ratio estimates available for analysis was somewhat less than 133 per person. Of course, the order in which the individual sheets were presented to subjects was varied to control for learning and order effects.

In addition to the distance estimates, other data collected included the familiarity of the subject with each location—this was indicated on a 4-point scale; sets of individual structural and functional variables such as age, sex, marital status, grade point average; and whether or not the individual possessed a car.

After estimates of cognitive distance were obtained, objective distances were obtained from street plans, using driving routes. For locations lying off the main north–south artery, several routes were generally possible. Because of the regular grid-pattern street layout in the area chosen, most distances were similar to within one-tenth of a mile. In cases where a number of different length routes were possible, the average distance over indirect and direct routes was used.

The data collected in this way were used to test hypotheses that had been partly generated in the formative 1968 study. The first hypothesis related to the directional biases of distance toward and away from downtown areas. It was also postulated that for an equivalent objective distance, cognized distance is greater for routes involving turns than for straight routes. These hypotheses are related to the notions implicit in the initial study, that cognized distances increase with, and are directly related to, the time required to traverse any given path. Obviously, as one moves off the major north–south artery, the potential number of turns in a route increases. Just as obviously, as one moves toward the center of an urban area, densities of population and buildings increase; the number of noticeable road intersections increase, as do traffic signs, stop lights, and so on. Consequently, the time required to traverse such paths would increase toward the downtown area, partly as a result of the occurrence of certain physical features, and partly as a result of an increase in the complexity of traveling. This would also influence cognized distances.

A preliminary analysis of some of the data collected in this latter experiment showed that for any pair of familiar and less familiar points located at approximately the same distance from a standard point, the familiar locations were perceived closer than those less familiar. Upon careful examination of the data, some convergence between objective road distance and cognized distance was found, as the distance between focal points increased. For small distances, cognized distances toward downtown were greater than those away from downtown. This study therefore supported some of the initial conclusions of the multidimensional scaling analysis conducted earlier.

Other investigators (Adams, 1969; Brown & Holmes, 1970) have studied the distance and directional biases of the movements of urban dwellers; and their results have tended to support the general conclusions drawn from these two studies. Further support has been collected, both from consumer behavior studies, such as those conducted by Lee (1968) and Rogers (1970), and from studies on other types of spatial behavior, such as the search for new residences prior to an intraurban migration.

Experiment 2

Perceptual Neighborhoods. The idea of a city neatly subdivided into "local areas that have physical boundaries, social networks, concentrated use of area facilities, and special emotional and symbolic connotations for the inhabitants" is the utopian dream of many urban analysts (Lee, 1963–1964, p. 16). In theory such areas constitute "a neighborhood." Attempts to recognize and define neighborhoods in urban areas have intermittently generated enthusiasm and despair among researchers. A lack of a consensual definition has neither prohibited the use of the term, nor diminished research into the origin, structure, and validity of the concept.

It is generally accepted that the neighborhood is something more than a geographically demarcated area. An essential element appears to be whether or not the residents of such areas perceive them as neighborhood units and perceive themselves as part of such units. Therefore we tried to determine how the inhabitants of a residential area identify with the concept "neighborhood." At first we concentrated on the problem of whether or not the subjective boundaries derived by a sample of individuals as a description of their neighborhood coincided sufficiently to allow the delimitation of a physical neighborhood space. Next we attempted to see if a social space could be derived which summarized local attachments and use of facilities. Then we examined the degree to which the physical space coincided with the social, or activity, space. We hypothesized that these combined social and physical spaces constitute a perceived neighborhood.

At the most elementary level, we can regard a neighborhood defined by a single individual as an area with which he closely identifies. Most individuals identify with others in their society who possess similar social and economic characteristics. The location of these "compatibles" frequently influences the choice of residential location. The possibility of the occurrence of groups of people with similar identity gives rise to the general notion that specific areas with similar populations can form in urban areas. The boundaries of these areas are sometimes unclear, usually consisting of a transition zone partially claimed and partially repudiated by adjacent core areas. Sometimes the identification of members with a particular core area or neighborhood is a function of a level of aspiration, rather than a function of actual belonging. This is supported, somewhat, by discrepancies between the extent of neighborhoods as perceived by those within an area and by those outside it.

As already suggested, a neighborhood consists of two component parts. The first of these is a social neighborhood which comprises the area in which an individual lives and interacts, and in which he involves himself with respect to finding friends and participating in community activities. The second is a physical neighborhood—an area capable of being delimited on a map and capable of being distinguished from the remainder of the urban area. Within this physical neighborhood, the individual "feels at home." In other words, the physical neighborhood is a segment of space with which an individual closely identifies. Lee (1963–1964) stated that physical and social spaces are inextricably linked in the mind of urban dwellers; and it may be impossible to separate the two. Keller (1968) also argued that the two spaces are indistinguishable in the minds of the residents. It is our contention that while these two component parts do correspond to a large degree, they can be distinguished; and that different sets of variables can be used to explain their spatial extents. Thus the major hypotheses tested in this study are: that neighborhoods can be defined by identifying the spatially overlapping social and physical spaces of a sample of individuals; and that specific sets of variables can be used to define the two component parts of the neighborhood.

To test our first hypothesis, a series of home interviews was conducted in an area known as Clintonville, an identifiable part of the city of Columbus, Ohio. Seventy-two subjects were chosen randomly from a residential area of approximately three square miles. Each resident was asked to draw a line on two separate maps: the first, to designate the physical area within whose boundaries the subject felt "at home"; the second, to bound the area in which his friends and acquaintances resided. In addition to these two areas designated on a local map, the respondents filled out an extensive questionnaire which summarized their degree of local involvement, their social class characteristics, life cycle, length of residence, and work place characteristics (see Table 3). They were also asked to identify, as closely as possible, where their friends and acquaintances lived, where they undertook local shopping and community activities, and so on.

Three basic analytical methods were used on the data collected. The first was map generalization, used to compile a composite picture of the social and physical neighborhood spaces as drawn by the sample respondents. The second phase was a *Q*-mode factor analysis to group sample respondents on the basis of their similarities across the sets of characteristics collected during the home interview program. The third phase was a multiple-regression analysis, using as a dependent variable the area of physical (designated) and social spaces, and using the questionnaire characteristics and some derived characteristics as explanatory, or independent, variables. In the last phase, only 50 home interview sheets were adequate enough for use in the regression analysis.

TABLE 3
Variable Listing by Dimension

Dimension A: Local involvement
Patronization of
1. downtown stores
2. shopping centers
3. local shopping clusters
4. commercial ribbon stores
5. convenience locations
   (near place of work)
6. home delivery facilities

Weighted figure based on number and distance of
7. friends living in Columbus
8. relatives living in Columbus
9. friends living in Clintonville
10. relatives living in Clintonville

The number of affiliations with
11. local organizations
12. city organizations
13. county organizations
14. stage organizations
15. national organizations

Dimension B:
16. social class

Dimension C: Life cycle
17. age

Number of children between
18. 0-5
19. 6-12
20. 13-18
21. 19-25
22. Occupational status
    (employed; unemployed;
    retired; student; housewife)
23. maritus status
24. sex

Dimension D: Length of residence
25. years in Columbus
26. years in Clintonville
27. years in same house

Dimension E:
28. place of work
    (distance from residence)

The Map Generalization Phase. Following a time-honored geographic tradition and duplicating the method used by Wilmott (1967), maps of the physical and social neighborhood spaces designated by the respondents were overlaid and summarized in an attempt to find the maximun and minimum areas designated by our sample respondents. Then, each set of separate maps was overlaid and convergence isolines were drawn. The percentage of maps in agreement and the spatial extent of the agreed upon neighborhoods is summarized in Table 4. For example, we see that 79% of the sample respondents designated a common area of .38 square miles as their social neighborhood; 81% of the sample respondents designated a common area of .45 square miles as their physical neighborhood. Ninety percent of the sample population designated the same 2.12 square miles as the area of their social neighborhood; while 96% of the sample responses designated a common area of 1.5 square miles as their physical neighborhood.

Maps of the physical and social neighborhood derived in this way showed that the two neighborhoods as perceived by the respondent are similar, but not exactly equivalent. In terms of the physical neighborhood, a slightly higher proportion of the respondents agreed on a common area. Note that in the social neighborhood, two central cores appear within the 6-block study area. Apparently a north–south residential street (Granden Avenue) provided some internal differentiation between the eastern and western segments of the sample group; but this minor differentiation was not as great as the two major arteries (North High Street and Indianola Avenue), which clearly define the eastern and western boundaries of the neighborhood. The influence of the two main north–south arteries, in terms of boundaries, is quite obvious; and is perhaps more obvious on the derived physical neighborhood, than on the

TABLE 4
Perceptual Map Agreement and Size

	Percentage of maps in agreement	Area (square miles)
Social neighborhood	79	.38
	7	1.38
	4	2.12
	10	4.00
Physical neighborhood	81	.45
	9	.88
	7	1.50
	4	3.87

derived social neighborhood. This may result from the respondent's tendency to think more in terms of accessibility, ease of movement, and concrete paths when thinking of the physical or tangible neighborhood.

The conclusions drawn from this map generalization study are twofold: both physical and social neighborhoods do exist in the minds of respondents and can be identified as such; and despite the fact that the physical and social neighborhoods can be distinctly identified, the degree of overlap is sufficient to warrant the statements made by other researchers, that the two are very closely linked in the mind of the urban dweller.

The Factor Analysis. The use of a *Q*-mode factor analysis enables the researcher to focus on the correlation of a series of persons, over a population of characteristics. Our aim in using this method was simply to find groups of people having similar social and spatial activity patterns. We then planned to map the location of these individuals and compare the resulting factor maps with those designated by individuals and used during the map generalization phase. This particular phase was quite successful in that three factors accounted for 90.4% of the total variance across our 72 respondents. The factors were identified by studying both the factor loadings and the response patterns of individuals in the original data matrix. If at least half the respondents with high loadings on a particular factor gave the same or similar answers to a series of questions, then those questions were used to interpret the nature of the factors.

Factor one was found to describe relatively young people with similar involvement characteristics. Factor two described respondents who showed great similarity in the distance relationship occurring with respect to their friends and relatives, and who were relatively new to the area (a resident of 5 years or less). Factor three grouped respondents who shared similar shopping habits, distance separation with respect to acquaintances and friends, and similar affiliation patterns. We consequently interpreted the first factor as a social factor, and compared the maps of respondents loading high on this factor with the area designated as the social space. The second factor was identified as a spatial factor and the maps of respondents who loaded high on this factor were compared with the extent of the physical neighborhood. Since factor three appeared to abstract parts of both the social and physical characteristics, no further attention was paid to it. We noted a high degree of consensus between the maps derived from the factor analysis and those derived from map generalization. Again, it can be noted that the maps derived from the factor analysis and designated social and physical spaces are very similar, but show sufficient differences to support the hypothesis that separate physical and social spaces exist.

The Multiple Regression Analysis. The hypothesis relating to the dimension of the areal extent of the neighborhood defined previously was tested using the sample data. A stepwise regression analysis was conducted with the area of the social neighborhood as the dependent variable, and 29 independent variables derived from the home interview questionnaire (see Table 3). Together the variables gave a multiple correlation of .79 (i.e., they accounted for 58.2% of the total variation). Among the intercorrelation

TABLE 5
Regression Output

Variables (in order of entrance)	R	R^2
Residence in Columbus[a]	.101	.010
Number of affiliations with city organizations[b]	.330	.109
Area of physical neighborhood	.391	.153
Relatives in Columbus	.428	.184
Place of employment	.482	.232
Age	.523	.273
Social class	.545	.297
Friends in Columbus	.595	.354
Friends in Clintonville	.624	.389
Relatives in Clintonville	.666	.443
Shopping center patronization	.680	.463
Occupational status	.687	.471
Number of affiliations with local organizations	.694	.482
Number of affiliations with national organizations	.701	.491
Number of children 6-12 years	.708	.501
Local shopping center patronization	.713	.508
Commercial ribbon store patronization	.720	.530
Home delivery patronization	.728	.530
Number of affiliations with state organizations	.738	.545
Number of children 0-5 years	.741	.549
Sex	.743	.552
Number of children 13-18 years	.746	.556
Downtown store patronization	.751	.563
Convenience patronization	.753	.568
Number of affiliations with county organizations	.756	.572
Number of children 19-25 years	.759	.576
Constant	.760	.578
Marital status	.762	.581
Residence in Clintonville	.763	.582
Residence in house	.763	.582

[a]Value significant at .99 level.
[b]Value significant at .95 level.

matrix variables, length of residence, social class, organizational affiliation, and the patronization of local shopping centers showed positive correlations with the social neighborhood area. The remaining variables, including life cycle, employment distance, and location of friends and relatives, were negatively correlated with the area of the social neighborhood. When examining the order of entry of variables into the regression (see Table 5), we noted that variables with definite distance characteristics enter early in the regression procedure, while personal, socioeconomic variables (such as age of children, sex, and marital status) were of relatively minor importance.

Efforts made to separate the physical and social neighborhoods, both perceptually and by factor analysis, appeared to be successful. There was sufficient similarity in the spatial extent of the two neighborhoods, however, to give some support to previously held notions that the two are so intertwined as to be indistinguishable in the minds of individuals. The slightly different configurations of each neighborhood space, however, does suggest that the two, while being similar in extent, can be distinguished. Our results also indicated that a relatively simple procedure of requesting individuals to identify physical and social spaces on maps is a useful and quick operational method of identifying these neighborhood areas. Certainly the degree of correspondence among the perceived maps, the output from the factor analysis, and the results of the regression analysis are most heartening. At this stage we also suggest further lines of research: larger and more detailed studies of neighborhoods; investigations of how neighborhood identification develops; analysis of the extent, shape, and number of neighborhoods within an urban area; and an examination of the theoretical shape and structure of the system of neighborhoods in any given city.

Experiment 3

Macro Studies. This experiment was conducted by Georgia Zannaras. The results are still being tabulated, and are not yet available in final form. The study dealt with four questions:

1. What environmental cues are utilized by individuals in the development of their mental image of cities?
2. Are the cues selected "structure specific"–i.e., are they the same for different city structures, or do they differ between city structures?
3. Does one type of city structure facilitate the development of comprehensive mental images?
4. What influence do variations in physical structure have on certain types of travel behavior?

In our attempts to answer some of these questions, we have conceived of urban environments as consisting of stimuli or cues, such as buildings, parks, and shopping centers, and supports, such as the paths used by individuals in their movement throughout the city. We argue that the cues and supports are associated in both a sequential and a hierarchical fashion. We suggest that observers will build their cognitive images from the existing environmental features by selecting and organizing those which are meaningful to them. When moving through the city toward some specific goal or location, the individual uses objective maps when his cognitive map lacks coherence.

One of the first aims of this research was to determine the types of cues used by individuals operating within urban environments. We suggest that a majority of these cues are fundamentally the same in all urban areas, regardless of their physical structure. However, the order of cues in the environment differs from structure to structure. Thus the sequencing, and perhaps the hierarchy, of cues which any individual can identify and use varies from city to city. Also, the occurrence of standard cues supports the notion of generalization of behavior from one city to another.

We also hypothesized that it may be the recognition of different sequential orders of cues and variations in the occurrences of hierarchical elements in urban areas which assist individuals in locating and operating within these areas. Furthermore, drawing on standard concepts in urban geography related to the frequency of occurrences of urban functions in places of different sizes we hypothesized that as city size increases and the frequency with which certain cues occur in the landscape increases (such as shopping centers, industrial parks, and so on), there is some change in the relative emphasis given to cues by individuals as they structure their cognitive images. Thus, as the frequency of occurrence of cues varies from city to city, the likelihood of selecting a certain city element as a critical cue to be used to anchor segments of a cognitive map also varies.

Our attempt at identifying environmental cues has taken place at two levels. First, a pilot study involving some 30 undergraduate students at The Ohio State University was conducted in an effort to make a list of the types of features which individuals use to help them operate within urban environments. This list was then supplemented by information from published articles (such as those by Appleyard, Carr & Schissler, and Lynch) which have considered the same type of problem. From a list of approximately 70 different features mentioned by our sampled respondents, 40 were mentioned by three or more. We compared these 40 with our list of features culled from published work; and determined a final list of 30 environmental cues (see Table 6).

TABLE 6

Environmental Cue Scale

P. Code Id. No.

Scales

When traveling to the center of the city, how important are the following features as guides to your movement? Define importance in terms of your remembering the feature in giving a stranger to the city directions for finding his way to the city center. *Circle* the number which you feel corresponds to the item's importance.

1. not important 2. not very important 3. indifferent 4. important 5. very important

1	2	3	4	5	1.	shopping centers	1	2	3	4	5	17.	neon lights in business areas
1	2	3	4	5	2.	railroad crossings	1	2	3	4	5	18.	rivers (streams)
1	2	3	4	5	3.	direction signs	1	2	3	4	5	19.	hills
1	2	3	4	5	4.	school buildings	1	2	3	4	5	20.	freeway system
1	2	3	4	5	5.	banks	1	2	3	4	5	21.	number and spacing of
1	2	3	4	5	6.	churches							freeway exists
1	2	3	4	5	7.	movie theaters	1	2	3	4	5	22.	industrial buildings
1	2	3	4	5	8.	restaurants	1	2	3	4	5	23.	public buildings
1	2	3	4	5	9.	open areas such as parks or	1	2	3	4	5	24.	residential quality changes
						green spaces	1	2	3	4	5	25.	residential density changes
1	2	3	4	5	10.	speed limit signs							(spacing of houses)
1	2	3	4	5	11.	the city skyline	1	2	3	4	5	26.	smog
1	2	3	4	5	12.	traffic congestion	1	2	3	4	5	27.	buildings become more
1	2	3	4	5	13.	traffic lights							numerous
1	2	3	4	5	14.	street width changes	1	2	3	4	5	28.	major dept. stores
1	2	3	4	5	15.	billboards	1	2	3	4	5	29.	slums
1	2	3	4	5	16.	bridges	1	2	3	4	5	30.	construction work

The scale of environmental cues (see Table 6) was constructed from a content analysis of the responses of our sample members; it included features such as isolated stores, shopping centers, dominant buildings, and signs. Once developed, the environmental cue scale was used at the second level of operation. It is currently being administered to a new sample of 150 subjects chosen from The Ohio State University in Columbus and its branch campuses in Marion and Newark. The purpose of this large-scale experiment is threefold:

1. To test hypotheses concerning the commonality of cues across different city structures.
2. To provide an idea of each subject's awareness of the environment for later hypotheses.
3. To provide information for structuring a selection of experiments relating to cognitive images of different urban areas.

It should be noted that the three urban areas chosen for large-scale experimentation differed substantially, in terms of their internal physical structure and size. Newark (Ohio) was selected as an intermediate-sized city which was largely sectoral in form. Marion is a much smaller city whose internal structure is basically concentric (in zonal terms). Columbus is a substantially larger urban area whose form might be described as one with multiple nuclei.

The purpose of the second level of this study was to examine a series of respondent's behaviors in various structured environments, through the use of both laboratory and field experiments. In particular, we hoped to support hypotheses related to whether detection of variations in city structure helps or hinders the development of cognitive images. A subsidiary problem was to find whether or not the cognitive images as perceived have any effect on travel behavior.

The second stage of this study aimed at collecting information from sample respondents in three ways. Initially each respondent was presented with several maps of each city. The maps were simplified land use maps, with six major categories of land uses. Each map had marked on it the occurrence of those cues which could be satisfactorily represented by symbols in two dimensions. Thus traffic lights, freeway intersections, open space areas, and so on were indicated on the maps. At first, each individual was posed the problem of outlining an effective pattern of travel for the purpose of obtaining a commodity found only in the center of the city. Records were made of the cues occurring on the trip selected, and also of ones which were not used. During the period of problem solution, respondents were asked to identify which cues they were using in order to select routes. In each case, the problem was to move from an external point to the city center. By comparing the performance of the respondent with respect to each of the structures, we hoped to obtain some indication of the degree to which the structure facilitated a particular type of spatial behavior—namely travel to the center of the city.

Having completed the nine trials with the maps of city structures, the respondents were then shown three-dimensional table models of the same urban areas. A similar set of tasks was then performed, with individuals being asked to move from a point on the outskirts of the city to the central business district and to record the types of cues they used to select specific segments of the route. Again the experiment was repeated three times for each city model, with the order of exposure to the table models being varied. At this time supplementary problems were also investigated. Sample problems included the following:

1. From several given alternative routes leading to the city center, mark the route that you would take if you desire to minimize the actual distance traveled.
2. Examine the selection of routes indicated on your model; all these routes are of equal length; mark the one that you would take to the city center.

We hoped, by using this type of task to determine the ease with which individuals handled questions and performed tasks, as physical structures of cities were varied and as the order and sequence of environmental cues also varied.

The final segment of the laboratory experiment involved presentation, in random order, of a series of slides to each subject. A total of 39 slides was selected for the three urban areas. Slides were chosen for their degree of representaion of different parts of the sample cities; and each slide included several of the cues mentioned in the environmental cue scale. Individuals were asked to identify where they were in an urban area, as represented by the features on the slide. This task aimed at determining if the subject could identify locations and land uses on the slide. A number of simplified land-use categories were provided on a separate sheet to assist in their interpretation. Subjects were also asked to identify the exact cues which they used in allocating each slide to a place in the urban area, and to rate the cues on a scale of importance. The scale values varied from 2 to 5, with 5 being the most important. Cues which were not present or were not used were rated "1."

In addition to identifying and rating cues, subjects were asked to estimate the distance between the place shown by the slide and the downtown area of the city in which it was located. This distance estimate was collected by means of a line scale. Subjects were given a scale with one-quarter of an inch equal to one mile; they were then asked to draw a line of a length representing the approximate distance that they thought the land use was from the downtown area. Those who were unfamiliar with the idea of drawing a line representing distance were asked to write the approximate distance. This last test depended on the range of cues present in each slide. It was both a test of the ability of individuals to recognize the cues, and a test to see whether or not different city structures facilated the development of knowledge about the city (i.e., whether or not the structural information presented in the set of slides increased or decreased the ability of individuals to correctly locate the slides within the given urban area, as the physical structure of the urban area altered).

The final stage of the experiment was a field study phase. Sample subjects from each of the three different urban environments were taken to preselected points in the urban area and driven over preselected routes to the city center. Each subject was exposed to two different directional routes: the first, from the periphery toward the downtown; and the second, from the downtown toward the periphery. Before undertaking the field trip, subjects were asked about their expectations as to what they would see on each trip. On the trip itself, they were asked to specify cues they observed along the way. After returning to the laboratory, subjects were asked to recall the cues in their appropriate order, from periphery-to-center or center-to-periphery, on each of the routes traveled. This phase of the study was completed with only a small subset of the total sample of subjects because of difficulties in arranging field trips in the three cities.

In essence, we used partly controlled laboratory experiments in an attempt to simplify some of the complexities of the "real world," and to help to see if variations in the physical structure of urban places determine some aspects of the conceptual structure of cities. This information was used to see if variations of the physical structure of urban areas influence certain types of spatial behavior.

Summary

To the nongeographer when perusing geographical literature, it must seem that geographers have attempted to explain overt or spatial behavior only in terms of the functional and structural characteristics of individuals and sets of existence variables, such as locations of the individual and locations of opportunity sets. Upon careful consideration, one is forced to conclude that geographers have probably accepted coincidental relations as explanations. In other words, they have found groups of individuals with similar functional, structural, or existence characteristics; have searched in the environment for some set of physical environmental factors which correlated highly with these individual characteristics; and then assumed some type of causal relationship between the two.

It is quite significant that geographers, in general, have little knowledge about the cognitive structures by which individuals operate; or if they do, then they have consistently ignored it. Realistically, we should be very unsure about the types of data that we collect by observing spatial activities, or by asking people what type of spatial activities they undertake. For the most part, the data which the geographer has used have been cross-sectional in nature, rather than sequential or time-oriented. If we take a cross-section of behaving acts in a randomly selected population, there is considerable uncertainty even as to the exact nature of the act which the people were performing at that particular time. In other words, it is not known if the act that was observed or recorded was part of a regular behavior pattern which could be described, repeated, and predicted with some degree of reliability. It could have been part of a random search procedure instigated by the individual in an attempt to find some satisfactory response; or a repeat of a previously tried situation which was on its way to becoming an established habit; or indeed a behavior which would *never* be repeated again! Traditionally the geographer has overcome these uncertainties by working with aggregated data and assuming that the data are truthfully representative of the way populations should act with respect to given objects. In effect he argues that if we take large enough populations, there is a high probability of finding acts which are repetitive, relatively invariant, and predictable. The degree of success enjoyed with some of the models developed in the past shows that this type of assumption is not entirely invalid.

However, our degree of confidence in our ability to explain spatial behaviors is probably much higher than it should be. This is simply because, for the most part, we really do not know what we are trying to explain. Our thesis in this chapter has been simply that by examining concepts of learning theory and concepts from such fields as perception, attitude formation, and motivation, we can begin to discover the nature of the data with which we principally work; and we can begin to gain some confidence in predictions we make for behaviors which can be identified as repeatable and predictable. Accordingly, though our work in environmental cognition and learning is very much piecemeal at this stage and probably badly formulated, we hope, in continuing this approach, to expand the relevant set of variables which the geographer uses in his attempts to achieve explanatory power—so that the geographer's predictions will gain more validity and his ability to produce relevant theory will also increase. Thus, while we have been using a diversity of approaches over the past several years, the experiments undertaken have been united by a common concern for the building of geographic theory which is logically sound, meaningful, and of considerable scope.

Chapter iv

Introduction

WILLIAM H. ITTELSON
ENVIRONMENTAL PSYCHOLOGY PROGRAM
GRADUATE CENTER
CITY UNIVERSITY OF NEW YORK

When faced with the comprehensive and overall treatment of very complex subjects which architects seemingly do almost by second nature, the psychologist tends to be somewhat at a loss for words. Chapter IV, "Learning from Las Vegas," is perhaps an outstanding example of this theme. The psychologist notes a number of separate topics, each one of which has traditionally represented a separate and extensive area of study within the history of psychology. Perceptual processes are represented by everything from simple localization in space, to complex motor behaviors in the context of the perceived environment. Cognitive processes, similarly, are represented by everything from the symbolic meanings of specific environmental objects, to basic environmental attitudes and underlying value systems. And this is not all: the entire rich field of human experience lies before the architect-observer and he eagerly harvests it all.

Therein lies the unique value of the contribution the architectural perspective can convey to the study of environment perception and cognition. The architect brings a quality of synthesis to the immediate occasion. He brings a global approach that recognizes that the whole is indeed much more than the sum of its parts. He moves, more or less at will, over the isolated details in an exciting and convincing effort to arrive at the essence of the situation which represents the deepest and truest level of meaning. But in the arena of the behavioral sciences, this approach is on alien ground;

it stands in sharp contrast to the writings which have preceded it in this volume. It does not require analysis, but the behavioral scientist finds himself almost irresistably compelled to do so.

Upon closer examination, three major psychological themes are found within this paper. They have already been briefly mentioned: first, the symbolic meanings of the environment; second, environmental attitudes and values; and third, overt behavior within the environmental context. In each of these areas, one is treated to the always fascinating and frequently brilliant insights of a group of architects as they themselves look at, experience, and study a particular environment. They report the messages they see transmitted by, and which they themselves receive from buildings, signs, highways, and parking lots. They express their attitudes toward, and feelings about, their experiences within this environment. Thus a rich, comprehensive, and convincing picture emerges.

What can the psychologist say which will add depth, or clarity, or coherence, or significance, or generality to this picture? First of all, he must applaud the dedication to understanding the world as it actually exists. The work here is not of self-appointed reformers having a view of how the world ought to be and a mission to make it that way. Quite the contrary: the world as it is, whatever that may turn out to be, is the subject matter. Here the psychologist wholeheartedly concurs; indeed this goal is certainly within the mainstream of historical psychological studies.

One might, however, ask of the architect the same question that the psychologist asks of himself: Do your findings, in fact represent what you are trying to find out? And here the basic difference in methodologies appears. To what extent can one safely rely upon the insightful experiences and analyses of a small group; and to what extent need one turn to the certainly less insightful, probably much lower-order, experiences of the large population to which one wants to generalize—information gathered by the careful and the rather painstaking procedures developed over a long period of investigation? One cannot help but wonder whether the exciting and brilliant comments in the following chapter are actually representative of a group larger than that of these writers and their colleagues. To ask this question is to suggest a possible program of study: to determine empirically the extent of the fit between the perceptions of the rest of the population and those which are described in "Learning from Las Vegas."

Having recognized the problem of the generality of the findings, one is immediately faced with a potential contradiction. On the one hand, whether the method be that of the architect or the psychologist, the goal is to describe and understand the world as it actually is, and not how it ought to be. But on the other hand, having found to one's satisfaction how it is, one must with equal care avoid the conclusion that how it is, is the way it ought to be. Since the buildings, symbols, and so forth so carefully analyzed in this chapter are actually found in the real world of Las Vegas, it is very difficult to avoid the assumption that they are there because people want them to be there and like them there; and to conclude that they ought to be there. In part this pitfall can be avoided by dealing with it as an empirical question in attitude measurement. However the more fundamental question of the implied value judgment remains, even though it is perhaps "introduced through the back door." This does not mean that the value judgment should not be made. It is rather to suggest the importance of knowing when the judgment is being made, and at what point in the analysis it can most profitably enter.

Perhaps the most important question which the analysis in the accompanying paper raises is: Having learned about Las Vegas, what has one learned about the rest of the country, about the rest of the world, and, indeed, about the rest of Las Vegas? Do Las Vegas and the supermarket actually reflect the basic values of our time? They certainly are "where the money is," but are they where our hearts are? Is their image one which has been imposed upon an unwilling population; or is it one that the population has in fact embraced and uses as an expression of itself? The experiences following the attempt by Venturi, Brown, and Izenour to base design on the analysis of Las Vegas and the supermarket suggest, at the very least, that what has been found is not an expression of the value systems of the people who perforce operate within it.

But whatever the "answer" to this question, the lasting importance of this study is that it has raised the question. This chapter is of particular importance for the issues dealt with, perhaps more than any so far presented, reach to the very essence of the relationship between the physical environment and the inner life of the individual. The basic concern is how and to what extent the physical environment functions, both as a reflection of the value systems of the people within that environment, and as an active component in the creation of those value systems. It raises questions, then, of the general principles underlying the relationship between the physical environment and human experience. These remain important questions which must be faced.

Learning from Las Vegas [1]

ROBERT VENTURI
DENISE SCOTT BROWN
STEVEN IZENOUR
VENTURI AND RAUCH, ARCHITECTS AND PLANNERS
PHILADELPHIA, PENNSYLVANIA

In this chapter we emphasize image over process or form—asserting that architecture depends in its perception and creation on past experience and emotional association, and that its symbolic and representational elements may often be contradictory to the form, structure, and program with which they combine in the same building. We argue for the symbolism of the ugly and ordinary in architecture, and for the particular significance of the decorated shed with a rhetorical front and conventional behind: architecture as shelter with symbols on it. We disagree with Modern architects in the Bauhaus tradition who shun symbolism of form as an expression, or reinforcement, of content; who say meaning is to be communicated, not through allusion to previously known forms, but through the inherent, physiognomic characteristics of form; who say the creation of architectural form is to be a logical process, free from images of past experience, determined solely by program and structure, with an occasional assist, as Alan Colquhoun (1967) has suggested, from intuition.

Purist Modern architecture developed partly as a reformist reaction against 19th century eclecticism. Gothic churches and Renaissance banks were

[1] Reprinted, with permission, from *Learning from Las Vegas*, Cambridge, Massachusetts: MIT Press.

frankly picturesque. The mixing of styles meant the combining of architecture with painting and sculpture. Dressed in historical styles, buildings evoked explicit associations and Romantic allusions to convey literary, ecclesiastical, national, or programmatic symbolism. Definitions of architecture as space and form at the service of program and structure were not enough. The overlapping of disciplines may have diluted the architecture, but it enriched the meaning. Las Vegas and the commercial Strip are the richest contemporary sources for this new, but old, direction in architecture.

Symbol in Space Before Form in Space: Las Vegas as a Communication System

All cities communicate messages—functional, symbolic, and persuasive—to people as they move about: *WELCOME TO FABULOUS LAS VEGAS, FREE ASPIRIN ASK US ANYTHING, GAS, VACANCY, WOW HAMBURGERS, GIRLS, GIRLS, NO COVER.* On the Strip the heraldic message system, the signs, dominate (see Figure 1); but two other systems are there as well: the physiognomic, the messages given by the faces of the buildings—the low, two-story structure with continuous balcony and picture windows on one side, and air conditioners protruding on the rear says motel without a second glance; and the locational—service stations will be found on corner lots. All three message systems are closely interrelated on the Strip and sometimes they are combined, as when the facade of a casino becomes one big sign, or the shape of the building becomes the sign (see Figure 2). Is the sign the building or the building the sign?

The Architecture of Persuasion

One of the ways in which we can deal with a new experience or environment is to place it in its historical context. We can regard the Strip as the latest evolution of directional commercial space which can be traced back to the Middle Eastern bazaar. The bazaar contains no signs; the Strip is virtually all signs. In the bazaar, communication works through proximity. Along its narrow aisles, buyers feel and smell the merchandise, and explicit oral persuasion is applied by the merchant. In the narrow streets of the medieval town, although signs occur, persuasion is mainly through the doors and windows of the bakery. On Main Street, shop window displays for pedestrians along the sidewalks and exterior signs, perpendicular to the street for motorists, dominate the scene almost equally.

Fig. 1. *The Strip, Las Vegas.*

Fig. 2. *World's longest sign.*

On the commercial Strip, the supermarket windows contain no merchandise. There may be signs announcing the day's bargains, but they are to be read by pedestrians approaching from the parking lot. The building itself is set back from the highway and is half-hidden, as is most of the urban environment, by parked cars. The vast parking lot is in front, not at the rear, since it is a symbol as well as a convenience. The building is low because air-conditioning demands low spaces, and merchandising techniques discourage second floors; its architecture is neutral because it can hardly be seen from the road. Both merchandise and architecture are disconnected from the road. The big sign leaps to connect the driver to the store, and down the road the cake mixes and detergents are advertised by their national manufacturers on enormous billboards inflected toward the highway. The graphic sign in space has become the architecture of this landscape. Inside, the A&P has reverted to the bazaar, except that graphic packaging has replaced the oral persuasion of the merchant. At another scale, the shopping center off the highway returns in its pedestrian malls to the scale of the medieval street.

Vast Space in the Historical Tradition and at the A & P

The A&P parking lot is a current phase in the evolution of vast space since Versailles. The space which divides high speed highway, and low, sparse buildings produces no enclosure and little direction. As a pedestrian, to move through this landscape is to move over vast expansive texture: the megatexture of the commercial landscape (see Figure 3). The parking lot is the parterre of the asphalt landscape. The patterns of parking lines give direction, much as the paving patterns, curbs, borders, and plantings give direction in Versailles; grids of lamp posts substitute for obelisks, rows of urns and statues as points of identity and continuity in the vast space.

But it is the highway signs, through their sculptural forms or pictorial silhouettes, their particular positions in space, their inflected shapes, and their graphic meanings which identify and unify the megatexture. They make verbal and symbolic connections through space, communicating a complexity of meanings through hundreds of associations in few seconds from far away. Symbol dominates space. Architecture is not enough. Because the spatial relationships are made by symbols more than by forms, architecture in this landscape becomes symbol in space, rather than form in space. Architecture defines very little: The big sign and the little building is the rule of Route 66.

Fig. 3. *Caesar's Palace, Las Vegas.*

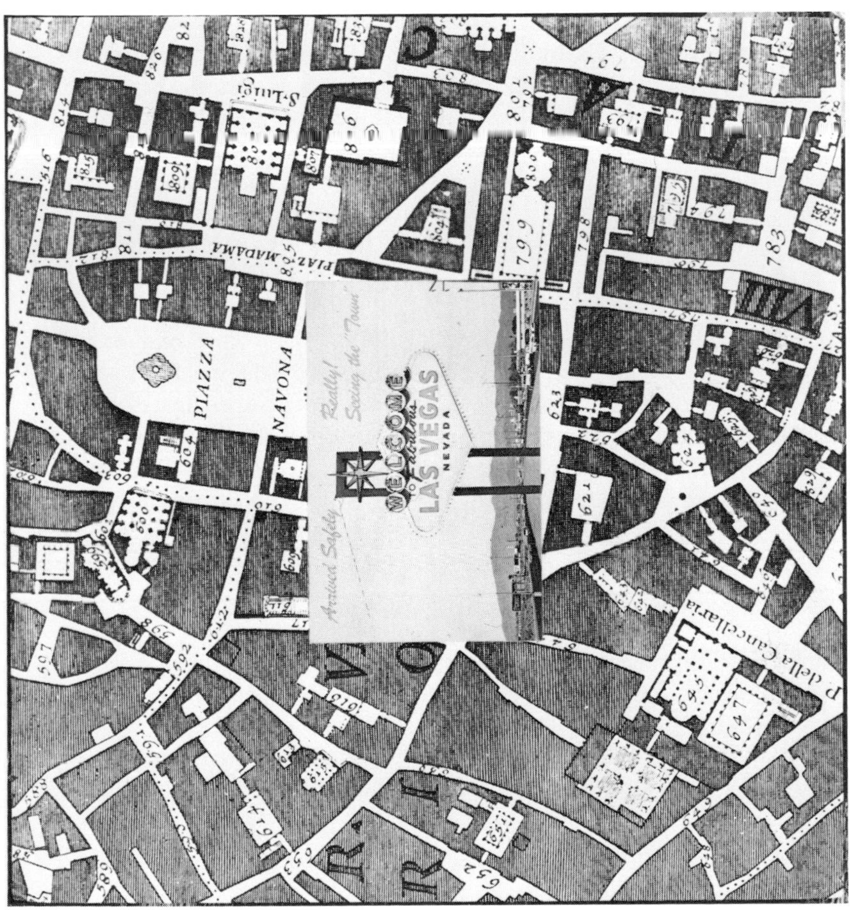

Fig. 4. *Detail, Nolli's map of Rome.*

From Rome to Las Vegas

Las Vegas is to the Strip what Rome is to the Piazza. Las Vegas *was* built in a day, or rather, the Strip was developed in a virgin desert in a short time. It was not superimposed on an older pattern as were the pilgrims' Rome of the Counter Reformation and the commercial strips of Eastern cities, and is therefore easier to study. Both Rome and Las Vegas are archetypes, rather than prototypes, and exaggerated examples from which to derive lessons of the typical. Nolli's tourist map of the mid-18th century reveals the sensitive and complex connections between public and private space in Rome (see Figure 4). Private building is shown in gray hatching which is carved into by the public spaces, exterior and interior. These spaces, open or roofed, are shown in minute detail through darker poche. Interiors of churches read like piazzas and courtyards of palaces, yet a variety of qualities and scales is articulated.

A Nolli map of the Strip reveals and clarifies the public and private domains in Las Vegas, but here the scale is enlarged by the inclusion of the parking lot, and the solid-to-void ratio is reversed by the open spaces of the desert. Separate mapping (redefined for Las Vegas) of the components of the Nolli map—asphalt, parked cars, empty space, building coverage, public space, public-private space—provides an intriguing cross-cut of Strip systems. Their reassembly gives Las Vegas' equivalent to the pilgrim's way, a linear Piazza, although, as did Nolli's map, it misses the iconological dimensions of the experience.

The Architecture of the Strip

It is hard to think of each flamboyant casino as anything but unique, and this is as it should be, since good advertising technique requires the "differentiation of the product." However, they have much in common, since they are under the same sun, on the same Strip, and perform similar functions.

A typical casino complex contains a building which is near enough to the highway to be seen from the road across the parked cars, yet far enough back to accommodate driveways, turn-arounds, and parking (see Figure 3). The parking in front is a token: It reassures the customer, but does not obscure the building.

The stylistic agglomeration of Caesar's Palace, Avis and Venus, Bologna's "Rape of the Sabine Women," and Flip Wilson, and the Strip as a whole approaches the spirit, if not the style, of the late Roman Forum with its eclectic accumulations of forms (see Figure 5). The high art original has been corrupted in an art historical sense, but its emotional, associative baggage

Fig. 5. *Avis and Venus. Caesar's Palace, Las Vegas.*

comes with it from the high source finally to the Strip. The association is Roman orgies; the message is basely commercial; the context is basically new.

Service stations, motels, and other simpler types of buildings, in general, inflect toward the highway through the position and form of their elements. Regardless of the front, the back of the building is styleless and physiognomically conventional, because the whole is turned toward the front and no one sees the back. The gasoline stations parade their universality. The aim is to demonstrate their similarity to the one at home—your friendly gasoline station. But here they are not the brightest thing in town and their signs are forced to new heights of physical size and illumination.

The Las Vegas Strip at night is symbolic images in dark, amorphous space. Any sense of enclosure or direction comes from lighted signs and the observer speeding along in his car, rather than from forms reflected in light. The source of light in the Strip is direct; it is the signs themselves, rather than surface reflections from external, sometimes hidden, sources as in the case with most billboards and Modern architecture. The mechanical movement of neon lights accommodates to the spaces at speeds our technology permits and to which our sensibilities respond. The tempo of our economy encourages the changeable and disposable decoration which is the advertising art in our environment. Architecture is no longer simply "the skillful, accurate and magnificent play of masses seen in light [Le Corbusier, 1927, p. 202]." Rather it is the masterly, correct, and magnificent play of lighted symbols in the void.

System and Order on the Strip

The Strip by day reads as chaos if you perceive only its forms and exclude its symbolic content and the effect of selective perception. The order in this landscape is not obvious. The continuous highway itself and its systems for turning are absolutely consistent. The median strip accommodates the U-turns necessary to a vehicular promenade for casino crawlers, as well as left turns onto the local street pattern which the Strip intersects. The curbing allows frequent right turns for casinos and other commercial enterprises and eases the difficult transitions from highway to parking. The street lights function superfluously along many parts of the Strip which are incidentally, but adundantly, lit by signs; but their consistency of form and position and their arching shapes begin to identify by day a continuous space of the highway, and the constant rhythm contrasts effectively with the uneven rhythms of the signs behind. This counterpoint reinforces the contrast between two types of order on the Strip: the obvious visual order of street elements, and the difficult visual order of buildings and signs. The zone of the highway is a shared order. The zone off the highway is an individual order. The elements of the highway are civic. The buildings and signs are private. In combination they embrace continuity and discontinuity, going and stopping, clarity and ambiguity, cooperation and competition, the community and rugged individualism. The system of the highway gives order to the sensitive functions of exit and entrance, as well as to the image of the Strip as a sequential whole. It also generates places for individual enterprises to grow and controls the general direction of that growth. It allows variety and change along its sides and accommodates the contrapuntal, competitive order of the individual enterprises.

Henri Bergson called disorder an order we cannot see. The emerging order of the Strip is a complex order. It is not the easy, rigid order of the fashionable high design urban renewal project. It is, on the contrary, a manifestation of an opposite direction in architectural theory: Broadacre City—a travesty of Broadacre City perhaps, but a kind of vindication of Frank Lloyd Wright's predictions of the American suburban sprawl. It is not an order dominated by the expert and made easy for the eye. The moving eye in the moving body must work to pick out and interpret a variety of changing, juxtaposed orders. It is the unity which "maintains, but only just maintains, a control over the clashing elements which compose it. Chaos is very near; its nearness, but its avoidance, gives . . . force [Hecksher, 1962, p. 289]."

Buildings and Theories

The complexity and contradiction among ordinary forms and symbols discussed here is, we hope, exemplified in the recent work of Venturi and Rauch. The theory and the work which follow do not necessarily correspond closely. Practicing architects tend to theorize inductively, starting with the concrete world around them, in our case with Las Vegas, Levittown, and historical architecture, and with their own current architectural problems. From these sources, working theories are derived. These derivations then temper the next work. Hence, what follows, being contemporary with our Las Vegas study, springs from the same views that sent us to Las Vegas, but does not correspond directly to them.

In any case, a building is a building and a theory is a theory. No architect should go all the way with his own philosophy, translating too literally this theory into his architecture, particularly into any one piece of architecture. That is too dry. But in a general way, this work shares much with Las Vegas, especially in its avoidance of the misplaced seriousness and humorless pomposity of current Modern architecture, which is not really serious enough, yet also lacks a sense of play.

Thousand Oaks Civic Center Competition, Thousand Oaks, California, 1969[2]

The competition program called for an initial stage, including City Hall and Chamber of Commerce, which was modest and restrictive in area and in functional relationships, and a second, looser phase which expanded the City Hall and added new departments and extra parking (see Figure 6). The community wanted a design in which "the individual having business with the city should be able to transact that business with the least possible waste of time, shuttling between offices," yet with a "certain dignity of expression and admiration," and a "permanent structure which will be likely to serve the community for upwards of a half a century.[3] By contrast, Thousand Oaks is a sprawling; growing, impermanent, California suburb. It is a city with few of the identifying characteristics of traditional urban forms of the East Coast or of a European city. It has grown in 12 years from a rural settlement of a "thousand oaks," and 2000 people scattered throughout the Conejo Valley, to an urban region of 50,000 "white collar, affluent, politically conservative and sixty percent Republican" citizens. The site chosen for the Civic Center was a rolling hill overlooking the Ventura Freeway between Los Angeles and Santa Barbara.

Our aim was in part didactic: The city hall should lead in demonstrating how the everday landscape can be enhanced using the practical tools at hand, rather than exotic and expensive imports. We tried to make civic architecture out of low, modest buildings, parking lots—symbols people like and can understand—and the signing systems they know from driving the freeway.

In a medieval town, a civic place is *defined* by the important buildings which enclose it. In a California suburb, a civic place is *located* rather than defined. Its location is marked by signs and symbolic images which can be perceived at high speeds across vast spaces of the highway, rather than by the modest buildings in big parking lots, outlined in the program. We sought signs and symbols related to the name of the community and traditional architecture of town halls. Town halls have towers and flags, and the "Thousand Oaks" are live oaks native to California.

Our building which is made of unassuming units of modular construction, designed for maximum flexibility and growth (a kind of camp Mies), changes at one ceremonial point, at the entrance to the council chamber. Here it evolves "poetically" from the same modular unit to form a tower which is a live oak and which becomes, in turn, a flag pole. On ceremonial occasions you

[2] This entry was developed in association with Tony Pett.

[3] Program for Thousand Oaks Civic Center Competition.

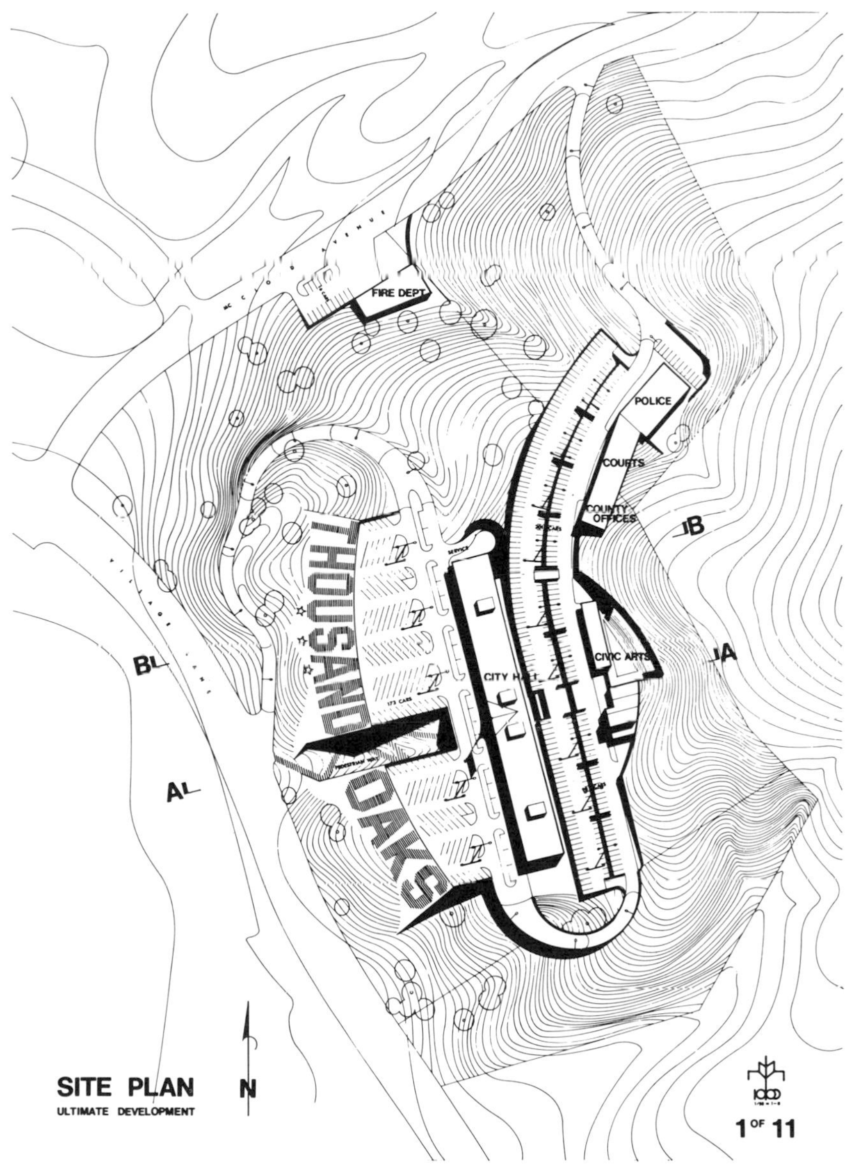

Fig. 6. *Site plan, ultimate development. City Hall, Thousand Oaks, California.*

enter the complex by walking under the live oak. The name "Thousand Oaks" etched lightly on the hillside berm resembles the efforts of high school children on other California hillsides or the flowered parterre of a Victorian court house. The words "Thousand Oaks" substitute a symbolic image of Thousand Oaks for a nonexistent civic skyline and for soon-to-be bulldozed oaks. The impact comes from the association of the words, and only secondarily from the architectural forms of another California suburb. Three small stars point up the larger meaning. All of the signs are to be read across vast space from moving cars, but are carefully detailed as part of the civic architecture.

Buildings and parking areas go with the contours, causing minimum intrusion on the landscape. Departments are zoned in functionally related groups, and each department is identified in tastefully lettered signs on the balconies and facias, to be read like today's special on the A&P windows. Buildings and automobiles are face-to-face as at the supermarket, to provide maximum accessibility to all departments for users. However, by twisting our "civic strip" up the hill and around a phony, flying freeway ramp in the second stage of development, we gave a sense of size and monumentality from the highway through superimposition. Moreover, by day the tree-tower is only lightly defined against its background, like a church tower. By night the live oak is etched in neon and will stand out small, but bright, against the dark hillside.

We regarded the parking as part of the civic architecture. Although monumental through its scale and size, it is terraced to the land to avoid excavation and has differentiated parking arrangements to suit different needs. We used the conventional elements of the highway—light posts, signs, curbs, ramps, and turning islands—to reinforce the urban reference. For the rest, we left the landscape untouched—a beautiful, bare California hillside.

Our design benefited from our experiences with Las Vegas and the A&P parking lot more specifically than we would want to expect in the developed project, since a building should be more than the embodiment of a theory. At least as important as the neon oak in this attempt to use the Strip vernacular civically, is the effort to civilize the parking lot. But our whole essay in suburban-commercial imagery was misdirected because this image was not the image Thousand Oaks had of itself. At the public showing our entry provoked comment: "It's cute, but are they really serious?" Perhaps a better point of departure, and at least as rich a source for inspiration and comment, would have been suburban housing rather than the suburban strip.

Chapter V

Introduction

HAROLD M. PROSHANSKY
ENVIRONMENTAL PSYCHOLOGY PROGRAM
GRADUATE CENTER
CITY UNIVERSITY OF NEW YORK

A psychologist is likely to encounter two difficulties with Chapter V. First, Field's analysis of the relationships between our changing health care system and its consequences for environmental design is wide in scope, highly trenchant, and extremely provocative in its implications for the behavioral scientist. Hermann Field, in effect, does not mince words, nor does he omit much. Second, and perhaps worse, is that there is nothing in his analysis with which one can disagree in any fundamental sense. For these reasons, this introduction is written from the point of view of "interpreter and synthesizer," rather than "critic and provocateur." However, I am concerned about some of the implicit assumptions to be found in Hermann Field's proposed solutions to the mismatch which now exists between the changing health care systems in urban communities and the institutional medical services and facilities in such communities. It is these assumptions which I examine in some detail in a major part of the presentation that follows.

To fully grasp Hermann Field's analysis of the problem of changing health care systems in relation to environmental design, one has to know something about Hermann Field himself, as an architect-planner. Two very significant characteristics are clearly and cogently revealed by his presentation. We see first a very real commitment to the *human scene:* to human dignity, and not just human life; to advances in technology not for their own sake, but for their capacity to realize the human potential; and finally, to environmental designs not as ends in themselves, but as a means of increasing, using Field's term, the match between the changing character of our society and human needs and satisfactions. In other words, he is committed not just to sound health care practices, the ideals of his profession, or the reality of urban life in a democratic society, but to the integration of all of them. Trite or not, it must be said the he is an architect-planner for whom people and their experiences have first priority in designing the urban health settings of today and tomorrow.

It may be asked, however, whether this is not true of most, if not all, architect-planners concerned with the environmental design of health care facilities. I am certain it is not, except in the very general sense that those in, and associated with, the medical professions must by definition be humane in their orientation. Indeed the broader credo—caring for the old, the indigent, and saving human lives—may cover up a welter of not-so-humane conscious or unconscious attitudes about how, when, and where health delivery systems should be established. The needs and satisfactions of human beings are as much rooted in the concept of *human dignity,* as in the concept of maintaining human life. In the environmental design of health delivery systems, it is easy enough to see architect-planners guided by principles more relevant to medical practice or process, innovative design orientations, or socioeconomic considerations, than to the feelings, attitudes, and desires of those for whom the health delivery system was designed.

If Hermann Field differs from other medical architect-planners in value orientation, then perhaps it can be attributed to the way he functions in this role. To use a simple expression, he works from the "inside," rather than the "outside." This, indeed, is the second characteristic of him as an architect-planner revealed by this chapter. As Director of Long-Range Planning for the Tufts–New England Medical Center for 10 years, Field is an essential part of the health care system he has been trying to modify and redesign, if not alter completely. He is not in effect a visiting consultant, nor an objective, detached, outside evaluation expert who, regardless of the number and length of the various briefing sessions, remains on the periphery of, if not outside, the human institutional setting he is asked to consider from an environmental design point of view. In other words, Field's grasp of the health care system he is attempting to redesign is based upon first-hand knowledge of the nature of the system, the kinds of people who are serviced by it and who give service to it, its larger environmental-community setting, the conflicting, as well as the congruent, values and attitudes of the various subgroups that make up the system, and so on.

It is agreed that even as an insider, no single individual can grasp all the ramifications and complexities of the institutional setting being redesigned. But no matter how limited the grasp of the insider, it is bound to go far beyond that of the external consultant, or outside evaluation expert. One might then raise the specter of bias versus objectivity, or vested self-interests versus detached, uncontaminated analysis. I would argue that the environmental planner, despite his direct involvement in the setting, usually can, and does, remain apart from it because by definition he is not an integral part of the health care system. He is neither doctor, patient, nurse, social worker, community health worker, union representative, or medical administrator. From the planner's point of view as a professional committed to a set of human values, it matters only that the health care system work, and work well, for all groups of individuals involved, especially those for whom it was designed.

It is important to digress here for a moment because Hermann Field's role as an insider has considerable relevance for the environmental psychologist or any behavioral scientist concerned with establishing the relationships between physical space and human behavior and experience. A New York City official who believes in planning and behavioral science research in solving some of the city's problems has spoken in disagreement with the way academic-behavioral science researchers usually go about attacking these difficulties. His complaint was that they move into the problem setting—and sometimes they do not get even this involved—do their research, and leave without any real commitment to the essential task of bringing about desired social change. The official was dubious about the contributions of these researchers because they seemed to remain aloof of the problem area itself: first, by not staying around long enough to fully grasp its complexity, which suggests less than useful and valid analyses of underlying determinants; and second, by avoiding long-range commitment and responsibility for helping to solve some aspect of the problem.

If effective environmental planning depends on community participation and the *long-term* involvement of the architect-planner, then perhaps effective behavioral science research requires the long-range participation of the researcher in which he assumes direct responsibility, along with the user, planner, and administrator, for bringing about desired social change. What is being suggested goes beyond Lewin's (1946, p. 39) dictum that social-psychological research must be socially useful, as well as theoretically meaningful, research, which he designated, as early as the late 1940s, "action research." Lewin pioneered the now increasingly accepted view that research on major human social problems cannot take place in the laboratory, or removed from the reality of the problem itself, whether the problem be juvenile deliquency, intergroup tensions, poverty, or the delivery of health services. But this is not enough. The grasp of the entire problem, its underlying determinants, and indeed the basic changes in the setting needed to ameliorate it and its consequences, require not a brief partaking of reality, but a *long-term* involvement and commitment to it. Increasingly it becomes patent that major social problems will only succumb to analysis and change when viewed, studied, and prescribed for by behavioral science researchers who are on the inside and are committed to stay there.

What is the problem? It is worth restating and not simply for purposes of discussion. Against the backdrop of his own long experience, Hermann Field reveals some basic insights into the American health care system, its limitations, and indeed the scope and complexity of the task of modifying it—modifying the health care system so that it better matches, or articulates with, the changing character of our society; or better said, with the changing needs, aspirations, and requirements of its citizens.

Over a period of at least five decades, the urban hospital has become the nexus for various dimensions of the practice of health care: bed care, teaching, research, outpatient treatment, diagnostic functions, rehabilitation programs, and more recently a concern with preventive medicine. In terms of the practice of curative medicine for the less than affluent, it has inexorably absorbed the role of the home, the physician's office, and the local pharmacy. By the same token, Field points out, "health care delivery is at a point of profound transition from this almost exclusive focus on sickness toward one of health maintenance as a societal obligation." Why can the transition not be made? One implication of Field's analysis is that modern medicine is neither ready, willing, nor able to make this change. He makes his point succinctly and precisely.

Having stated the general problem, Hermann Field then points out the significant problem areas of the hospital complex which confront the planner; following this analysis he presents the indispensable characteristics of any future American health care system; and finally he specifies the environmental facility requirements needed to implement these basic changes in the health care system. There are particular points in these three major sections I wish to consider, especially with respect to their implications and the implicit assumptions underlying their acceptance.

Field states that for the hospital planner a serious problem is the hospital's lack of response for change—its special knack for built-in obsolescence—brought about by a clinging to old conceptions and practices, a production time lag of 5 to 10 years, and a constantly accelerating change in which sudden discoveries in medicine or drastic shifts in financing have differential, as well as unpredictable, consequences. Thus, he points out that "the hospital planner must seek to minimize facility concepts and growth patterns that will narrow future options," which in turn raises the whole question of "permanence versus readily disposable or convertible facilities." In other words, space and its facilities must be designed for *flexibility*, both in terms of varying utilization patterns and open-ended growth possibilities. Obviously, there are many design issues involved in establishing the flexible building structure or, as Field notes, what John Weeks calls the "indeterminate building."

Apart from the issues concerning just what kind of design concept will permit the most effective rational growth and reutilization alternatives, there is an important underlying assumption in the design approach which seeks to maximize future options that Field, Weeks, and other architect-planners will have to come to consider very seriously. Indeed we offer a simple dictum: Regardless of what architect-planners intend in the design and present and future use of a physical setting, the realization of these intentions will ultimately depend on those individuals who administer and/or make use of the setting.

The design approach which seeks to maximize future options rests directly on the assumption that individuals, groups, and the administrative and functional structures which sustain and organize them in the hospital system will, in fact, be ready to use these environmental planning options when the time comes. A necessary and critical concomitant of facility concepts and growth patterns which maximize future options in the design of the hospital is an administrative system, a role structure, and indeed a value and attitude orientation of the individuals involved which will facilitate and implement a choice among these options when the time for such a choice arrives.

From the viewpoint of the behavioral scientist, a fundamental theoretical issue is involved here. Inducing changes in attitudes, values, behavior, and practice at the level of the individual, group, or institutional setting is no simple matter. Even where options exist to the extent that particular design, health, or human relations problems can be ameliorated, these options frequently have not been used. Behavioral scientists have grappled with, and conceptualized, the nature of social change and its induction; but, as yet, our understanding, and therefore our ability, to initiate and guarantee desired social changes in attitudes, behaviors, and practices is highly limited.

Hermann Field implies the importance of this factor in the present American health care system when he alludes to the built-in obsolescence of the hospital, and which he attributes to "the use and the reuse of retrospective standards that have accumulated in agency and architects' files and the minds of administrators . . . and the general tendency of institutions to keep on replicating that which has proved itself acceptable in the past." But what this statement does is merely describe, and not explain. Nor can obsolescence be attributed to such simple sovereign principles as "inertia," "maintaining the status quo," or "what is familiar is more desirable than what is unfamiliar." The factors—at all levels of social organization—that resist change now are no less likely to inhibit such change in hospital settings which maximize future design options, unless appropriate steps are taken to modify the attitudes, values, behaviors, and practices of all the human groups involved.

And in this regard the users of the health care systems must not be overlooked. Thus Field is essentially right when he suggests, early in his presentation, that it is primarily institutionalized medicine which stands in the way of the needed transition from a curative to a preventive medical health system. But I wonder if the role of the patient, or citizen, and his attitudes and values about medicine, his own health, and his role in a health care system can be ignored. If the modern urban hospital is not responsive to change, neither is the patient. Whether the problem is smoking and cancer, annual physical examinations, health education offerings, or venereal disease—and many more examples can be given—Americans need considerable indoctrination in the need to prevent illness rather than to rely on the doctor's cure after falling ill. As long as the user of the health care system is *unwilling* to think about his own well-being *before* it is threatened, then indeed institutionalized medicine can easily afford "to turn its back on how to avoid such sickness."

Let me repeat my essential point. Even if John Weeks finally establishes one or a number of optimum physical designs for his "indeterminate building," their ultimate success will depend on the social, attitudinal, and value systems which organize the activities of the individuals who will be contained by them.

In a highly perceptive discussion, Field explores the question and stresses the need for systematic research on the effect of the hospital complex on the individuals who use it—in terms of its scale, technology, and complexity. I would be hard put to find a better supporting rationale for much of the psychiatric ward and hospital research undertaken by those of us in the Environmental Psychology Program at the City University of New York (Proshansky, Ittelson, & Rivlin, 1970). By the same token, Field also reflects on the limits imposed on this type of behavioral mapping research and related empirical procedures by such factors as age, sex, cultural and ethnic variations, changes in patient's perceptions over time, sudden shifts in administrative practices and/or medical personnel, and so on.

When he turns from the hospital itself to the impact of the hospital complex on its surrounding community, Hermann Field provides a fundamental insight in emphasizing, simply and directly, that what is good for the growth and development of the hospital complex may not be good for the community in terms of its other institutional needs and requirements. Indeed, to quote Field, "The mere scale and power disparity can be seen as deeply threatening." What is true for the hospital is no less true for the university in the fairly common "town and gown" conflict.

What makes Hermann Field's analysis in this particular respect most compelling is the fact that despite systematic attempts to avoid such an outcome, through careful planning and design concepts for his Medical Center, it occurred anyhow with respect to Boston's Chinatown. This community was, and is, threatened by the new hospital complex despite all precautions taken. The question is: Why did this happen?

It may well have been that after two previous invasions of their "territory," no amount of planning could have reconciled the Chinese community to the development of a medical center in their midst—particularly, as Hermann Field suggests, when in subsequent years growing tensions between the older and younger generations of Chinese in the community made the Medical Center a convenient focus for externalizing these in-group antagonisms. Indeed it may have been absolutely necessary for the Chinese community to find such a *common enemy* in order to prevent its disintegration because of a struggle for power between the young and the old.

Whatever the reasons for the alienation of the Chinese community, a number of implications follows from the analysis given, with respect to the planning process. First, it is important to stress that an institutional complex exists not in one community, but in as many communities as there are distinguishable ethnic and social groups involved—groups whose past history, place in the social status system, level of assimilation into, or acclimation to, the larger society, and geographical location differ from each other. If, as it has long been recognized, the nature and extent of minority group prejudice depends on the particular ethnic or racial group involved, it is probably no less true for the reasons just given, that they will differ in their responses to the plans, aspirations, and intentions of the dominant group in the community.

But an even more important implication can be drawn from Hermann Field's experience with the Chinese community. Long-range planning of physical facilities which takes into account the needs of the community and its members; the social and economic consequences of the proposed facilities; and its effects on other institutional settings can be only as effective as the stable characteristics or conditions of the community which guided the development of the newly proposed environmental design. Like a physical facility, a neighborhood or community does not exist in a vacuum. The neighborhood, too, has a larger context which may exert influence on it to the extent that it may change either temporarily, or irrevocably, in fundamental ways. There was no way to foretell the sudden and quite recent immigration from Hong Kong into the Boston Chinatown which brought about a land and housing crisis whereby the Medical Center was viewed as a powerful and voracious competitor for much needed space in the area.

Here the significance of Hermann Field's earlier observation becomes apparent: that rational solutions to design problems at a given point in time may later result in mismatches between facilities and activities because of administrative practices and/or personnel change. Solutions to problems of the relationships between the hospital complex and the community are no different.

Following his analysis of the problem, Field turns to a discussion of some essential characteristics which will be, in his judgment, an indispensable part of any future American health care system. In brief, it must evolve as a national health insurance program which provides comprehensive, decentralized health care, focused on preventive rather than curative medicine, under the auspices of medical teams involving physicians and a diversity of other highly trained personnel, including social workers, computer experts, and technicians. One could not agree more with Field's general prescriptions for the future, although as already suggested with respect to the shift from an emphasis on sickness to health maintenance or the prevention of such illness, changes of this kind will not come easily. And upon closer examination of the kind of facility environments suggested by Field to implement these fundamental changes in the health care system, many problems arise with regard to some of his implicit assumptions about people, their attitudes and values, and the nature of social change.

Field presents us with 11 characteristics of the environmental setting of the hospital required to implement his proposed changes in the American health care system. Basic perhaps to all the rest is his proposal that the new hospital environment must take the form of "decentralized modalities of care housed in essentially small-scale, less complex environments." He uses this characteristic—which he lists first—as the nexus for all the rest. He indicates how the specific properties of this new kind of hospital environment are to be determined, how it is to be used, what virtues will ensue as a consequence for the individual and the community, and what other characteristics it must have to achieve a maximum return. In addition to the first characteristic he cites, there are three others which deserve special comment.

Field points out that these new, decentralized, small-scale environments "must be developed as an outgrowth of a participatory process with the consumer community to make them truly effective environments." It is important to stress that there is a deceptive and appealing simplicity to the community-participation approach which belies the many problems confronting the planner, architect, or even social researcher who uses it. Hermann Field's experience with Boston Chinatown makes this quite evident. We have already noted two problems: first, a community may consist of many social or ethnic groups whose differing, if not conflicting values, attitudes, and life orientations make it difficult to achieve consensus; and second, communities are also subject to external influences—sudden economic and political stresses at the national or state level may engender conflicts in the community which will make its significant institutional structures, and any attempts to change them, subject to strong attack.

A third problem involved in community participation probably caused the most difficulty between the Tufts–New England Medical Center and the Chinese community. To the extent that the particular community group lacks both political and economic power and its own resources, and indeed has a different life style, including a language difference, the community-participation approach to environmental planning and design decisions will provide very limited returns. Sharing in the decision-making and planning process is merely a first step. A second, as Hermann Field suggests, is putting the health care facility in the consumers' environment and making it an integral part of their lives. But to truly achieve the second step, the group involved must have the power, the personnel from among its members, and a sense of being *equal* partners in the larger venture with the other groups involved—equal not only in decision making, but also in knowledge, authority, resources, and professional and administrative status.

That the community at some significant level of grassroots participation must be involved in the planning process I do not dispute. What concerns me is the level of this involvement. In terms of broad value decisions, the community membership should be allowed to decide the general nature of its own existence in terms of economic priorities, the character of its physical setting, and whether indeed it should give up a large parcel of land for a major hospital complex or a new town industry. On the other hand, I question the validity of community participation at the level of the design itself, where decisions have to be made about specific locations, structural forms, communication systems, and so on. What concerns me is the erosion of professional competence in favor of a "democracy-or-bust" approach: Whatever "the act," we all get into it. Decision making in design and planning is difficult enough for the architect-planner considering that he must integrate various types of technical, social, economic, and, at times, political data, without turning it over to those least equipped to make such decisions. Community members are no more competent to make these decisions than they are as local school board members to decide the specifics of the curriculum and the kind of teaching methods to be used.

For the architect-planner to turn to, or allow, the community to provide solutions to his own very difficult technical problems is an abrogation of professional responsibility. In matters that require the rational analysis of complex problems, what the people want is seldom what they need or what is good for them.

Hermann Field specifies that the new small-scale health facility "should be able to reduce institutionalization to a minimum and maximize psychologically supportive characteristics in the environment, with strong health educational inputs." And earlier he specifies that these settings *will be* "responsive to change through such factors as low investment (disposability), or demountability. . . . Thus, the tendency of activities to become slaves of the rigid facilities which dominate them can be reversed. . . ."

I fully agree with these two environmental design recommendations and indeed all of the others made by Hermann Field as a means of implementing the radical changes he proposes in the American health care system. I suspect, however, that my strong agreement is in part of function of the very considerable similarity, if not identity, of my value orientation to health care with his. As a behavioral scientist, however, I find myself less certain about some of his recommendations because they rest on assumptions about people and their behavior in relation to settings which can be *challenged.* In this sense I take on the role of "devil's advocate," as a means of sharpening Hermann Field's environmental design recommendations for implementing his proposed health care system. I cannot fault him for his failure to deal with these issues because, after all, he is an architect-planner, not a behavioral scientist.

The crux of Hermann Field's approach is decentralization as a means of achieving "essentially small-scale, less complex environments." Taken with his various other recommendations, they are seen as a means of achieving a health care system to match the changing character of modern urban society. Yet it is important to note that the four fundamental features of this system specified by Field: a national health service; emphasis on health maintenance;

a social and economic, as well as organic, orientation to health problems; and a comprehensive, integrated, and easily accessible health system are by no means inherent in the environmental design recommendations he makes. That is, there is nothing inherent in the centralized, complex, urban hospital system which precludes a national health system, comprehensive (although not easily accessible) in its emphasis on the prevention of illness, and which involves health orientation which is economic and social, as well as organic, in character.

Yet, it is true that inextricably woven into the fabric of his discussion of the four features of tomorrow's health system, Field is stressing a fifth, and perhaps more fundamental, feature: The health care system must be humane; its critical focus must be the person, not just as a patient, but as an individual whose total well-being has first priority.

Is decentralization and the resulting small-scale, less complex health facility module the best way to achieve this significant objective? Like Field, I think so, but there are a number of issues which confront us immediately. Between the programmatic statement and the reality of the existence of such units are many unanswered questions about the form and direction the small-scale, decentralized hospital should take. From the point of view of *physical design alone*, it is not simply a matter of "small size and less complexity," but a host of other properties in relation to these general dimensions with which we have to deal. Improperly conceptualized and subsequently realized, the decentralized module system can be as much a mismatch as our present system.

The issue just raised is clearly revealed in considering Field's eight environmental design recommendations. He specifies that these facility environments should be able to reduce institutionalization to a minimum and maximize psychologically supportive characteristics in them. The problem can be stated simply and directly: We know too little about environmental design and its influence on behavior to be able to design our small-scale community health setting to bring about these effects. However, even if we did have this knowledge and acted on it, we would still be far from the humane health care system envisioned by Field. Willingly or unwillingly, he seems to make the assumption that given decentralization and the appropriate small-scale health facility setting, the rest will follow. However, a psychologically supportive environment in which institutionalization is reduced to a minimum may depend only partly, perhaps even minimally, on the design of the physical environment.

What troubles me is that planners will plunge ahead with these new, small-scale units—putting them in the local community, making them unobtrusive, integrating them into other institutional settings, and so on—and yet not know the nondesign ingredients which will make them work. One is reminded that millions of dollars have gone into the construction of open schools—or schools without walls—during the past five years, and yet many of them are providing far less than was promised because of the nondesign ingredients: Teacher attitudes, articulated educational programs, and proper guidelines for use were considered after the fact, and not before.

There is evidence throughout Chapter V, albeit implicit, rather than explicit, that Field is aware that a humane, manageable, hospital setting will depend on more than just design considerations in the form of a decentralized, small-scale health facility. He is sensitive to the need for special kinds of personnel, a new way of training physicians, and health education with respect to illness prevention. Yet what he omits is perhaps far more critical than all other physical and social design considerations; namely, the nature of the social system which will organize this decentralized, small-scale, diversified health care structure.

The attempt to achieve minimum institutionalization, a personal, rather than an impersonal, health care practice—one which will be responsive to change—will require a corresponding reordering and redefining of the values, attitudes, and expectancies of the various groups of individuals who participate in the health care system. In other words, the proposed physical changes in the system can be effective only if the social system and the individuals within this system think, act, and believe in ways consistent with the proposed objectives of the health care system itself.

Before the system can really work, doctors, nurses, paraprofessionals, clerks, patients, secretaries, social workers, nurses aides, and others will have to do a great deal of relearning. Each of these participant groups, or at least their successors, will have to learn the new health care system. Training and educational programs will have to be modified; changes in the medical hierarchy and in the structuring of roles will have to occur. The personalization of human relationships depends not only on the properties of a physical setting in which individuals can interact with each other on a one-to-one basis, but also on how their relationships to each other are defined by their immediate role situations and the larger social system of which they are a part.

As I consider Hermann Field's analysis of the American health system in its entirety, and his recommendations for change, I suddenly become aware of the importance of "not throwing out the baby with the bath water." The importance of this adage is revealed in two ways by his presentation. First, nowhere in his paper does he consider in any detail the positive aspects of our present health care system, particularly with respect to retaining centralization where its validity as an administrative, organizing concept is greater than that of decentralization. Indeed he as a planner and I as a behavioral scientist must continue to consider the problem of how to make large, centralized, institutional hospital complexes more humane and psychologically supportive, if in fact other issues of higher priority require such a system over the small-scale, decentralized approach.

In this sense it is quite critical to remember that the environmental design criteria which Hermann Field has evolved on the basis of his proposed new health care system are probably most appropriate to the large urban settings where poverty, ethnic prejudice, and severe social class distinctions are commonplace. Obviously it is just these settings that constitute the "problem of the cities" confronting America today. It may well be that for smaller communities, where these problems are less severe, the small-scale, decentralization approach to health care may be less appropriate. Although Hermann Field discusses facility types, I believe he is referring to the question of variation within large urban centers. The important factor to be emphasized is that the design implications he draws from his radically conceived health care system reflect not only the properties of this system, but also those of the type of the community setting he has in mind, namely, the large urban community. Variation in the size, group composition, social structure, and life style of the community may require a change in the final set of design implications specified by Hermann Field. It is conceivable that in other types of communities a centralized, rather than a decentralized, environmental system may best implement the new health care approach suggested by him.

Environmental Design Implications of a Changing Health Care System

HERMANN H. FIELD[1]
DEPARTMENT OF POLITICAL SCIENCE
TUFTS UNIVERSITY

The area of environmental cognition is a no-man's land lying between the physical settings with which the design professions seek their corner on immortality and the behavioral sets which threaten instant obsolescence to these same creations. Whatever label we place on this disputed territory—environmental psychology or the sociophysical environment or man–environment systems—it represents an indispensible resource for understanding the limits and potentials of design manipulation in relation to human activity.

As an architect, I am increasingly baffled by the arrogance of my profession in its commonly held assumptions as to the benign quality of facilities that consistently increase the nonhabitability of our man-made environment. The fact is that among many other more obvious indicators a growing body of investigation in the social and behavioral fields points to a fairly pervasive mismatch between the facility and the activity needs which are supposed to justify its existence. And worse still, we cannot blame the mismatch simply on change, for it is usually built-in right from the start.

[1] Formerly Planning Director, Tufts – New England Medical Center.

My 10-year focus on the replanning of an urban, teaching, medical center has brought home to me the many ramifications of this mismatch, so conspicuous throughout the present American health care field. Thus it is a particularly rewarding area for investigation, albeit a painful one if you are also saddled with the responsibility of implementation. The only hope lies in a holistic planning and design strategy, meshing at whatever level possible the changing health care system with its behavioral, social, and economic matches into a designed environmental outcome. Here I am speaking not just of cognition of specific designed spaces or buildings, but also of the larger perception by a community of the institution in its midst. This image is fraught with a lot of cultural history, of past actions and present grievances which finally congeal in the explosive mix of confrontation slogans. It is useless to respond by saying that they are distortions, or even direct misrepresentations, for they are very real to those involved. Such concerns can be met only by a nonalienating approach to planning and design capable of merging such patterns of cognition within the synthesis of user and professional collaboration.

The Present Picture

The approach to the subject of health care requires initially a quick look at the state of the art in the United States, the raw material available as a starting point for anyone in planning or design manipulation of the environment in which such care takes place. Our health care system (or is it actually a nonsystem?) could well be summarized—paraphrasing Arthur Schlesinger—as "our American high standard of low care."

This trait seems to repeat itself at numerous levels: in the mix of superb facilities for intervention in life-threatening situations and overt sickness, matched by an abysmal ineffectiveness in the prevention of disease; in huge and ever-growing expenditures on hospital services and doctors' fees, coupled with exceedingly unequal locational and economic access to health care of uneven quality; in a pile-up of biomedical technology and specialist skills, side-by-side with makeshift primary care; in ever greater emphasis on organ pathology and on disease episodes, while ignoring the human and environmental setting which may be contributing factors; in ever larger and more costly building complexes, increasingly removed from sites of everyday activities; in services and policies imposed on a user community which is deprived of direct participation in their formulation and operation.

The Traditional Sites of Care

The focal point of the health care system, and its most dominant element, is the hospital—the bellweather of the institutionalization of present-day health care and policy. With its overwhelming preoccupation with disease and curative medicine; its monumental investment in buildings based more on past models, than on the present ones (let alone future models); its growth pressures that become a threat to the fabric of its surroundings, the hospital reveals within itself most of the critical elements which beset the health care system as a whole. So an examination of environmental design implications of a changing health care system might well start with the role of the hospital. But first, what other elements of care has the hospital come to dominate?

Traditionally, of course, though unofficially, the home has been the main site of health care. This probably still is the case today—certainly in the areas of minimal, chronic, and even much of terminal care, since of some 1.2 billion days of bed disability annually in the United States, 600–900 million take place in the home. This role was reinforced by the visiting physician and a degree of other supportive services from outside the home. At the same time, the home setting has been one of the main causative parameters for overt sickness. Worsening housing conditions, increased mobility, and the shrinkage of the traditional family nucleus, as well as a growing middle class affluence which could provide a comfortable, institutional surrogate for the home have all contributed to a downgrading of home care, as has the end of the era of the general practitioner with his little black bag. Correspondingly, a second site, the physician's office, has grown in importance, mainly in relation to minor treatment and diagnosis requiring a minimum of supportive equipment. Certainly until recent decades it has been the main clinical setting for the average American.

In turn, with increasing specialization and the concomitant importance of diagnostic hardware, the one-man general practice began to disappear, especially in urban areas where it was prohibitively expensive. Meanwhile, in suburban areas, from a clustering of physicians into private group practice clinics, a new office setting has evolved. However, this setting has been largely inaccessible to the less wealthy members of American society. Though the burden of health care cost has been somewhat lightened by partial, third-party coverage, the group practice is strictly a market place, fee-for-service operation, rather than one based on need.

Again quite unofficial, a third site for care is the ubiquitous drug store, both for self-medication and for the pharmacist's ever-ready, free consultation. The pharmacy is actually the second most heavily visited health facility, with over 2 billion prescribed medicines passing over the counter in 1970. A fourth site is the so-called nursing home, in its many variants—usually a fairly crude profit venture, a repository which keeps chronic and terminal patients out of sight and concern, primarily offering custodial supervision and only secondarily paying lip service to nursing. As a consequence of longer life expectancy and the degenerative diseases associated with an aging population, the nursing home has become a major adjunct to the system, as well as a disgrace. Hopefully, modifications are emerging in some of the newer variants, such as the so-called extended-care facilities.

Meanwhile, the hospital itself has shifted its character and role considerably over the past half-century. While still overwhelmingly concerned with disabling sickness and emergencies, it has absorbed functions provided by the other traditional sites, as well as developed a whole new range of capabilities in curative medicine that has grown out of the biomedical advances of the past decades. Thus, the original, exclusive emphasis on bed care has been almost equaled by the development of diversified treatment facilities and support services, and in the larger teaching centers by massive research components.

Utilizing these new resources also for clinical treatment of ambulatory patients has effected a further shift in the system. While large, urban hospitals traditionally provided a site for minor clinical treatment, primarily for the medically indigent, outpatient care was at best a secondary service, absorbing only minor resources in staff and facilities. In the post-World War II period, with the great increase of diagnostic skills and treatment hardware, the vertical patient began to receive increasing attention at the hospital site which, in effect, became an upgraded surrogate of the traditional, physician's office. Thus, the movement has been toward even greater gathering of all curative, as well as diagnostic, services under the mantle of the hospital, creating a unique concentration of specialist skills and treatment facilities toward the conquest and amelioration of sickness. As part of these expanded functions, the hospital has also begun to enter the field of preventive care, or health maintenance, with facilities for check-ups and follow-ups. It would seem then, that in the future, health care will be centered around the hospital as the best-suited universal locus. Certainly in dollar expenditure, facilities investment, processing capacity, and professional resources, the hospital has become one of the major economic forces and power groups in the American economy.

Then why do I suggest that the hospital, as presently conceived, conceals an increasingly critical environmental mismatch, one with which the planner and designer of health care facilities must come to grips?

The Hospital Mismatch

It is the hospital which today serves as the primary setting for health care. Thus the most important factor to consider is: What is happening to the concepts of the health care which the hospital is supposed to serve? Over the centuries, organized health care successively concerned itself with putting away the victims of wars, isolating those who could spread infection from the healthy body of society, and providing a place of last resort for the chronically disabled poor. More recently, the hospital has also undertaken, in a major way, general nursing and supportive treatment in acute sickness; now, as the more well-to-do take advantage of such services, there is a corresponding effort to supply environments and services closer to those of a hotel.

Today, however, health care delivery is at a point of profound transition from an almost exclusive focus on sickness, toward one of health maintenance as a societal obligation. No doubt American society has the capability of making this transition. Essentially, all that is lacking is the will to do so and the development of the alternative system components with their facility environments and organization.

As in so many other aspects of American life, it is mainly upside-down priorities which stand in the way of effecting changes in the health care system. Meanwhile the crisis deepens; only the time dimension is in doubt. Medical costs skyrocket. The average person does not enter the health care system until much irreversible damage has already occurred, both impairing the quality of life and incurring unpredictable, and often catastrophic, costs. Such a system is extemely expensive and hardly compassionate. Yet overwhelmingly, institutionalized medicine continues to turn its back on how to avoid such sickness. Almost the entire outpouring of money focuses on treatment after the event—and no wonder, with the deadweight of hospital tradition in the driver's seat, with the huge investment in facilities, with manufacturing, professional, and service know-how all geared to curative medicine. In this sense, the hospital has unwittingly become one of the major impediments to redirecting our knowledge and capacities into innovative channels. Here lies the basic mismatch between the institution and the changing system of health care delivery.

From this mismatch a chain of further considerations for the planner and designer is derived. Is the hospital perhaps obsolete, both as institution and setting? Until this issue can be in some way clarified, should a moratorium be declared on all further hospital construction, as the province of New Brunswick, Canada, did recently, for nearly 2 years? (This freeze on hospital construction was to enable a comprehensive province-wide study of actual needs. According to the Llewelyn-Davies, Weeks, Forrestier-Walker, & Bor partnership who undertook the study, considerable capital and operational savings have already become apparent since resumption of construction. In the area of highway construction, a similar moratorium has been imposed upon the Greater Boston area while a new, socially and environmentally oriented, and balanced transportation solution is under study.) Alternatively, toward what modifications should the planner be working to make the hospital a more viable environment in this period of transition? What directions in change and growth are specifically suggested? And what analytical tools are available to the design professional in his search for environments most supportive to new activity sets that have none of the long institutional traditions behind them? These are some of the questions that need to be resolved.

Main Problem Areas of the Hospital

With radical shifts in future health care in mind, what are some of the main problem areas within the hospital which the planner must face? Beyond doubt—it is almost a platitude by now—the biggest problem is responsiveness to change. It must be emphasized, because even in relation to past and present problems, the hospital has shown a special knack for built-in obsolescence. This derives in part from the use and reuse of retrospective standards that have accumulated in agency and architects' files and in the minds of administrators; from restrictive funding programs; and the tendency of institutions to keep on replicating that which has proved itself acceptable in the past. As a result, there has been a continual tinkering and attempt at updating concepts which may have long since outlived their usefulness. The tendency to turn to the equipment industry, waiting in the wings for ever greater investment in hardware back-up as a substitute for software benefits, is a contributing factor. Another built-in handicap is the production time lag of 5 to 10 years in the present fund raising–planning–design–construction sequence required to produce a functioning facility. This is due, in part, to the unusual complexity of hospital design, but even more to the profession's inability to provide quick-response methodology.

The main factor, however, is the constancy of accelerating change. A hospital is a very complex mix of many lines of change which are unlikely to move at the same pace and which may be affected by sudden discoveries in medicine, or by drastic shifts in financing mechanisms, such as the introduction of some form of national health insurance. A breakthrough in cancer prevention or therapy would have a radical effect on surgical bed use and the need for radiotherapy services. On the surface, a major, national thrust in the direction of health maintenance would increase the hospital's ambulatory requirements, as opposed to the acute care sector. But again, it might have the opposite effect. A decentralization of such preventive care services out into the community might, in actuality, relegate to the hospital only those ambulatory care procedures requiring a high level of diagnostic and treatment back-up.

Meanwhile, the early decades of health maintenance are likely to reveal a large volume of previously neglected overt sickness. This, in turn, might put increased pressure, for some time, on hospital beds, before ultimately reducing the need for them. Pending a more accurate knowledge of likely cause and effect and the crystallization of major national policy decisions, the hospital planner must seek to minimize facility concepts and growth patterns which will narrow future options. Here, questions of permanence versus readily disposable or convertible facilities are evoked.

John Weeks (1964), the British hospital architect, has put a major emphasis on this in his search for the "indeterminate building." This of course relates not only to ability for reuse alternatives, but also to open-ended growth. The bigger the complex, the greater the danger of locking out rational growth altogether. For example, concentric growth out from a core creates ever greater imbalances between the center and the periphery, as is known from city growth. It can be countered only by an initial overdimensioning of the core and a fingering process outward, allowing for later filling in of the interstices, at considerable cost in underused communication lines in the early stages. One alternative is a linear approach with repeating circulation nodes. Here distances become a problem, however, and interaction among parts is greatly impeded. A positioning of elements at right angles along a circulation spine, similar to the concept of the old, American, army camp hospitals, provides a greater freedom, but requires adequate land to grow upon. Growth along a grid of multiple circulations creates a more compact model without need of a core, leading in its most confined form to a kind of megastructure.

I would like to take up another problem area facing the hospital planner today, one closer to the subject under discussion. In the long road of adaptation from earlier, relatively simple, and small-scale functions to the huge hospital complexes of today, what has been the effect on the human users of the environments that have been created? What, for example, is the impact of scale? Has the increased reliance on technology introduced negative responses? Is the institutional atmosphere overbearing, and if so, how can we ameliorate it through the planning process and design? Patients tend to be regressive under the anxieties of hospitalization. Should the environment be supportive to this plunge, or should it seek to counter it by spaces which enforce independence and self-reliance? In fact, what are the limits of direct therapeutic impact of physical design? Does anybody really know? How much is consciously perceived, how much subliminal? How much is indirect, through design-induced organizational and operational changes which in turn affect the user? This is an area where few hard data are available.

Architects think in terms of process flow, of arrangements for operational efficiency, of equipment or furnishing for specific activities, and of cost benefits. They have not been attuned, or trained, to the nature of behavioral response, and either ignore it, or conversely impart their designed environment with exaggerated human benefits. Most of the recent attempts at analysis in this respect seem to have been associated with the space program and research into survival in hostile environments.

One attempt to work with behaviorally oriented design directives was undertaken in our own planning at the Tufts-New England Medical Center, in research on the pediatric hospital environment (Kreidberg, Field, Highlands, Kennedy, & Katz, 1965). We observed the negative impact on children of the linear rows of rooms with a corridor on one side and windows relating to nothing in particular on the other. This found expression in the following design directive:

Beds should be so placed that children can relate to the internal environment even more than the external environment.

Because:
1. The child is more interested in activity involving people than in a distant view.
2. Children in bed require something to hold their interest and compensate for their immobility.
3. Children tend to put emphasis on peer group interaction.
4. This kind of placement allows the patient to orient himself to an informal play area.

Except:
1. where the parent is totally involved in the care of the child while in hospital
2. where the degree or type of illness requires intensive nursing care and/or privacy
3. when the age of the child is such that tactile communication is more important than visual communication

Starting out with a simple statement, "Children want to see and be seen," coupled with their evident need to relate and participate, we developed a cluster concept of patients around a central activity area balanced by a similar external courtyard or patio between clusters. Thus, informal community settings were created in place of the linear impersonality (see Figure 1). This same concept was later carried through into the design of the adult inpatient facilities, making possible greater flexibility in use, as well as a much more interactional adult environment (see Figure 2).

Fig. 1. *Hospital design for children.*

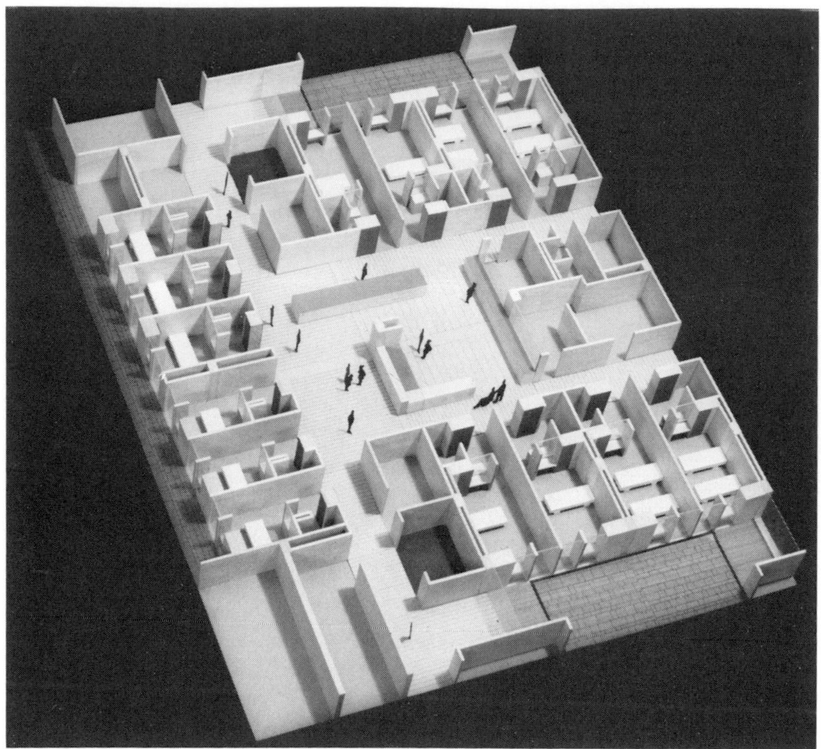

Fig. 2. *Hospital design for adults.*

But how do we know that the desired outcome is achieved and that it is effective in the sense intended? This brings up another major responsibility in any effective planning and design, that of the evaluation of designed environments in their actual use. The fact is we do not have, at present, reliable tools to test performance in behavioral terms. As a result, we are caught between safe obsolescence and the danger of fadism, the so-called latest solution. Actually such evaluation should be developed for a number of stages in the planning and design process, to check out alternative routes and to make corrections ahead of involvement in the huge investment of the completed facility. Enlistment of the techniques of human factors psychology opens up some avenues, as do the various time–distance tracking of personnel, patient, and materials movement. Computer-aided evaluation and simulation is likely to become another significant tool. However, a much broader approach will be needed, including a better knowledge of intangibles less susceptible to management, such as the fluctuations of the patient's cognition during the various stages of his treatment or illness, the impact of cultural, ethnic, and socioeconomic factors, of age, and of sex. Still another element is the instability of the institution itself. How can we compensate for discontinuity in administrative policies or shifts in the main medical actors? While a design may have been a rational solution given the actors at one point in time. it may turn into a sharp mismatch later if not used within the context intended.

But even as we develop a sounder methodology and greater ability to cope with the planning and design aspects of the internal hospital environment, only part of the problem is solved. A facility does not exist in a vacuum. Presumably there is a neighborhood of some sort around it, which may even have been part of the reason for creating the institution. A community's well-being, however, does not just relate to matters of medical care, especially if its provision has been locally marginal in relation to the specific institution. The community's conscious focus is more likely to be on employment, housing, education, self-identity, territoriality, and security. Unwittingly an institution, in its focus on a particular mission, may fail in other respects of equal, or even greater, concern to its surroundings. Especially in an urban context, essential growth needs of the institution may be in direct conflict with the physical, social, and even economic survival of its neighborhood. The mere scale and disparity of power can be seen as deeply threatening.

In fact, this is the 1972 reality for the Tufts–New England Medical Center and Boston's Chinatown—in spite of 10 years of painstaking work to develop a planning strategy and design concept which would minimize this kind of outcome. I would like to dwell on the relationship between institution and community in more detail, as it is a telling element of the urban hospital's cost–benefit balance sheet. In the case under discussion there is a special irony in that the approach toward the neighborhood had, over the years, been cited as an outstanding example of responsible and enlightened planning, in contrast to the Newark or Harvard Medical or many other urban institutional expansion programs. And so it was, in terms of 1961, or even 1967. But what was acceptable then is seen in a very different context today.

In 1961, I coupled the recommendation that the Medical Center stay in downtown Boston's blighted South Cove on our 10 acres of hopelessly fragmented land, with a renewal strategy for this 100-acre neighborhood that would revitalize its vanishing residential base. Thus we developed a growth strategy based on consolidation through rational land assembly and high utilization, with a minimum of outward expansion. A long-term, 15-acre growth limit was visualized, a mere 50% above the total site of that time, sub-sub-minimal as compared with the 50-, 100-, and even 150-acre stake-outs of other medical centers across the country. Feasibility was premised on two

Fig. 3. *Project within a project: South Cove renewal area and Medical Center development plan.*

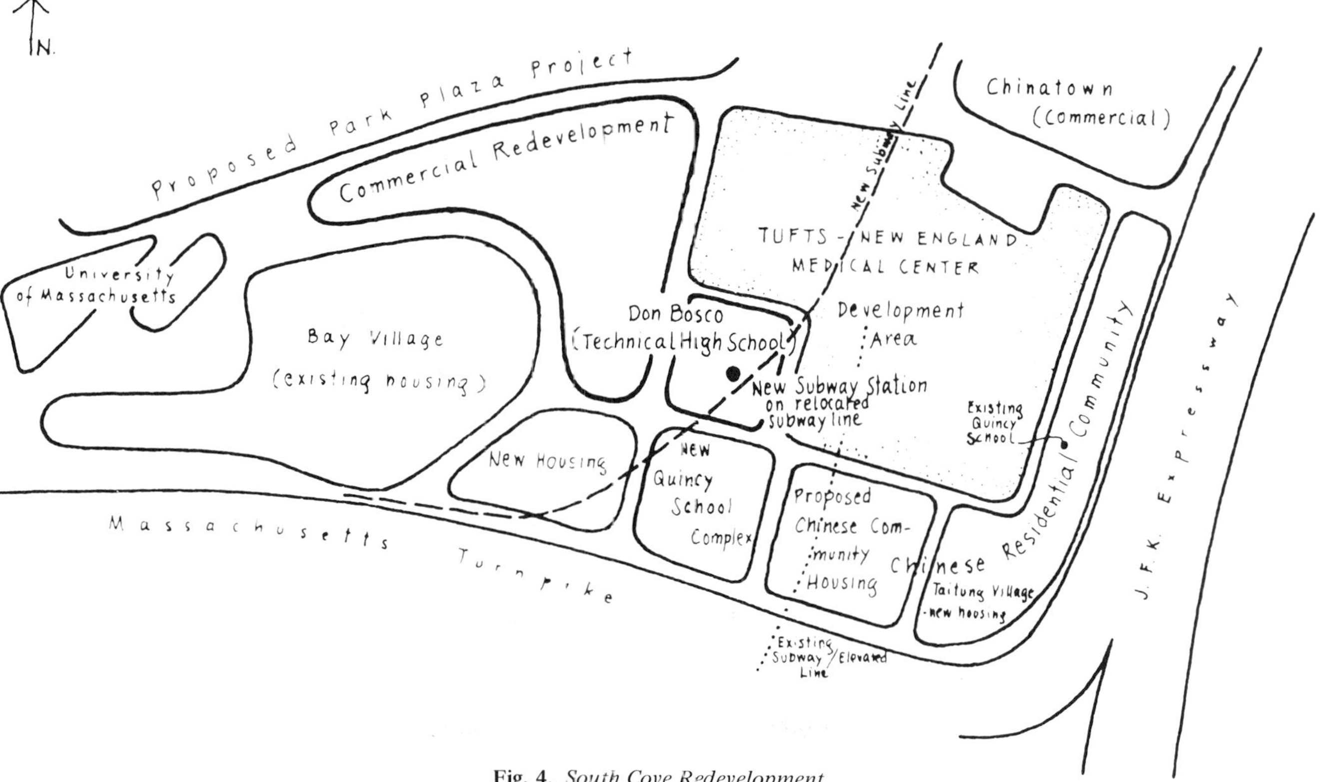

Fig. 4. *South Cove Redevelopment.*

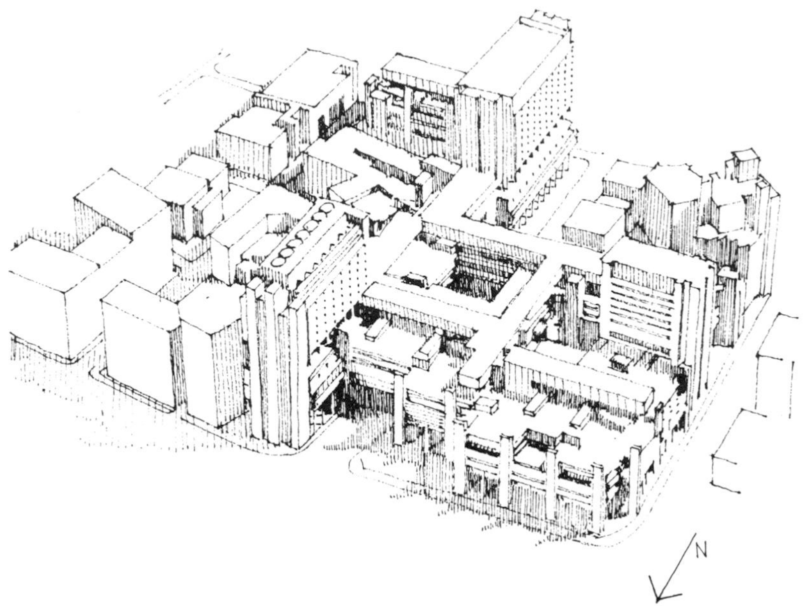

Fig. 5. *Tufts-New England Medical Center.*

main assumptions: that we could develop a much more intensely interactive design concept than was possible with traditional separate building entities; and that on-site hospital growth would, over the next decades, taper off in favor of decentralized components out in the community. To soften the scale barrier of the proposed continuous megastructure (see Figure 5), we floated the Medical Center over a shopping plaza, pedestrian walkways, and even the main downtown street of Boston with a new subway station under it. Thus we created a whole new potential activity area at the center of our neighborhood. Furthermore, we pushed the main growth direction away from what was left of the Chinese residential community after years of intruding institutional expansion and major highways which had twice bulldozed through it. The city's renewal plan for the area returned some land acquired by the Medical Center to the community to enable the Chinese to sponsor their own moderate-income housing project, completed in 1972. Also, it created a demarcation line for future land use between neighborhood and institution which would protect the former from future encroachment. The demarcation line was agreed upon by all parties concerned.

Meanwhile, we sponsored a major development effort for a new public elementary school to replace one built over a century ago (see Figure 6). Our goal was to create through it a community resources center. As a second activity focal point, it would, through the device of multiuse joint occupancy, attract to itself major recreation facilities, community activity spaces, a day care center, a model school health program under Medical Center sponsorship, a family health clinic as a first, experimental, off-site modality, a little city hall, and housing. The housing initially designated for open occupancy

Fig. 6. *Existing 125 year-old school.*

was subsequently changed for use by married students of the Medical Center, when the original idea became unattainable (see Figure 7).

The project, with extensive federal and foundation research and development funds, also brought into being, under community pressure, a first participatory organization. This community council lost no time in making clear that the institutional paternalism of the early 1960s was gone, and that planning the Quincy School complex and its services was primarily the responsibility of the community. The past 2 years have been a rocky road for all concerned, but in the upshot we are all a little wiser, more flexible, and more realistic, and the project is moving toward construction, though only in truncated form.

Meanwhile, however, crisis broke out with our Chinese neighbors—there was an awakening of the Chinese community into this part of the century, a phenomenon not confined to the Chinatown of Boston. Internal tensions between older, traditional power and younger challengers found a convenient externalization in the long past of grievances and the presence of domineering institutionalism in their midst. The highway people were gone (see Fellman & Brandt, 1971) and nothing would bring back what had been destroyed. But the Medical Center was a different matter. Overbearingly visible, it quickly

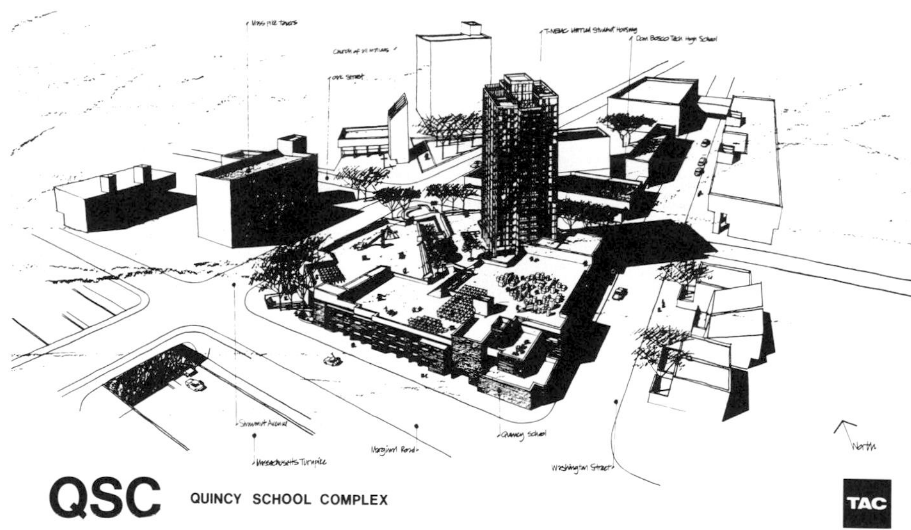

Fig. 7. *Perspective view of Quincy school complex, showing rooftops, play areas, and housing tower.*

became the focus of an equivalent of the Black Power protests of the 1960s, albeit in a quieter Chinese version.

While a cornerstone of planning policy had been toward a multiethnic community, representing also its white, black, and Puerto Rican constituents, the Chinese saw this as eroding their identity. For them, there was only one community—theirs—and one battling for survival from a politically weak and economically impoverished position. As a result of the sudden immigration from Hong Kong in the late 1960s, there is a rapidly worsening land and housing crisis, with no place for neighborhood growth in an already crowded area. No wonder the Chinese have turned to a roll-back strategy directed against our 15 acres, minimal to us, but huge in the eyes of a hard-pressed resident who finds himself in the shadow of this alien monster.

An excerpt follows from a flyer headed, "Stop Tufts!" The flyer was issued by the Free Chinatown Committee (May 12, 1971), and found its way to every front door in our area.

> A struggle, which has already lasted over 30 years, is still raging below the calm of Chinatown. This struggle between Tufts New England Medical Center and the community has brought Chinatown to the edge of total destruction. . . This self-interest-seeking institution, in alliance with the city, has stripped us of our land and has destroyed at least 650 of our homes without replacing a single unit of housing . . . we demand of T-NEMC: An end to all and any further T-NEMC expansion now and a commitment to replace, with low-income housing, all housing destroyed by previous expansion.[1]

This issue, more than grievances in the health sector, and in spite of all efforts toward conciliation, brought us belatedly to the brink of a confrontation and presented a serious threat to the hospital's present and future services, teaching and research capacities.

Our past and present failures to meet the primary health needs of our immediate neighbors have not gone unnoticed, but have also become an explosive issue. To again quote the flyer produced by the Free Chinatown Committee:

[1] I might add that the flyer ignores actual history: only 38 units were Chinese owned or tenanted, of a total of 111 units acquired in this period, all on the open market, many beyond rehabilitation due to dangerous settlement. The neighborhood was primarily Syrian and Lebanese until the 1950s. It was highway construction that produced massive destruction through the heart of Chinatown and was a prime factor in the southward push of the neighborhood into the immediate proximity of the medical center.

> . . . Tufts-New England Medical Center health services are inaccessible and unacceptable to the community because of:
> –language barrier and lack of interpreters;
> –cost-fees for services at Tufts discriminate against low-income populations;
> –a history of racist treatment of Chinese patients at T-NEMC;
> –hostility created by ruthless land acquisition. . .

Especially for such a threatened minority community, impersonal institutionalism is one key impediment to effective care, as is inequality in power, professionalism and resources. While accentuated by special conditions in the case of the Tufts–New England Medical Center, this barrier is an ingredient in most hospital–community relations.

The question arises whether a hospital can fulfill a responsible mission in such circumstances. What is the ultimate balance sheet? What portents are there here for the centralized hospital complex as a viable base for future inner-urban care? I suspect that only through new routes whereby the community becomes an equal partner in health care planning, and eventually emerges as the client contracting for health services on its own terms, will a basis develop for more effective health care on the community level.

Toward a New System of Health Care Modalities

The next issues to consider are the postulated alternate kinds of future health delivery systems and the environmental design criteria which can be formulated to guide those engaged in planning appropriate facilities for them.

What are the principal characteristics missing in American health care today which will be indispensible to any future system?

1. The system must be comprehensive and nonredundant, with easy access to each level of care; it must provide continuous, integrated coverage. A cornerstone will be the development of health care networks in place of the nonsystem of haphazardly placed hospitals providing fragmented services. Of course, hospitals will remain as key nodes of such a system in a gradual process of restructuring their functions and relationships. Various networks have existed for many years in other advanced industrial countries, usually on the classical pattern of a hierarchy based almost entirely on hospital components. An early attempt at regional systems in this country has been the Bingham Program in northern New England, radiating out from the Tufts–New England Medical Center all the way to small, rural outposts. The United Mineworkers provided another early hospital-based model.

A more recent system is the Community Mental Health Centers Program of NIMH with a broad range of categorical modalities: inpatient services, outpatient services, partial hospitalization (day or night care), emergency treatment, consultation and education, diagnosis, rehabilitation, precare, aftercare, training of professionals, and research and evaluation services (Glasscote, Sanders, Forstenzer, & Foley, 1964, pp. 7–8). Here is a blueprint for a total system; yet the system is, in effect, deficient for it relates to only one aspect of the health spectrum and thus emphasizes a new fragmentation. Significant, too, is its statement of aims: *(a)* to locate facilities reasonably near the patients' homes; *(b)* to provide a comprehensive range of services; *(c)* to make services both immediately available and easily accessible; and *(d)* to provide continuity of care until restoration or rehabilitation is completed (Glasscote *et al.*, 1964, pp. 29–30). While emphasis is still primarily on the treatment of mental illness, rather than on its prevention, the statement of aims reveals, in intention at least, many of the elements likely to appear increasingly in the years ahead.

2. Future American health care must redirect human and economic resources from sickness toward health maintenance. This can be done without impairing present capacities in curative medicine, where, except in a few selected areas, increasing investment is bringing correspondingly lower returns in relation to earlier periods. The refocusing of the health care system involves a concomitant redirection of medical education toward social medicine, to produce more physicians capable, and desirous, of entering this area, thereby increasing overall physician manpower.

3. A majority of incipient health problems are as much social and economic as organic. They require skills broader than those the physician is presently trained to supply. His special knowledge can benefit many more patients if he is relieved of work others can do as well or better. In fact, part of the ineffectiveness of present health maintenance efforts is the inability of the physician, with his specialization, to act effectively as broker in the complex issues of preventive care, or even be interested in them. He is neither ideologically nor professionally qualified to play this role. Health care responsibility must shift from the closed preserve of the medical practitioner to the health care team in which the physician functions as key member in a collaborative effort with nurses and physician surrogates, or categorical specialists, similar to the Army's medical corpsmen, technicians, and social workers. The growing enlistment of computer and video technology opens up further possibilities of greater manpower effectiveness. William Schwartz (1970) has written of the computer-aided physician substitute in tandem with circuit-riding supervisory physicians. All of this points to the need for a large range of nonphysician training programs, with a deliberate effort being made to obtain such manpower out of the employment pool of the catchment areas

concerned. In this way, a much more responsive link between user and service and a sense of identity with the community would be created.

4. The future health care system must remove all economic barriers to health care. This can be achieved only through some form of national health insurance which will provide for health maintenance as a societal right, as well as full protection in the event of catastrophic or chronic sickness. This would also have to include a shift to prepayment, rather than the present market place fee-for-service structure, to assure that the individual is not penalized for his efforts toward health maintenance; and that the system is provided with built-in economic incentives toward minimizing sickness and keeping bed occupancy down. Such prepayment, in one form or another, is the practice in most insurance schemes abroad, whether through a national health service, or a mix of more traditional carriers. In this country, isolated, earlier efforts which were fought ruthlessly by the medical profession, through the American Medical Association, have more recently been followed by a number of experiments, such as the Harvard Community Health Plan, in many cities across the country. The most successful model, of course, is the Kaiser system, with its continual efforts at refinement and innovative exploration (Garfield, 1970). I would like to dwell for a moment on the thrust of this specific model which introduces a number of new features. Among other considerations, it recognizes the increasing jam-up of patients at the point of entry into the system. At present, effective channeling mechanisms are lacking. There is no real way of sorting the well from the sick, while distinguishing all the gradations in between. With a major shift toward health maintenance, there will be a huge increase in this unsorted flow into the system, mostly of persons with no visible ailments, or with primarily non-medical ailments.

As a first step, the Kaiser system introduces the so-called multiphasic screening center. With the aid of highly sophisticated and automated testing equipment and chemical autoanalyzers in a streamlined processing system, a health profile is put together in a single patient contact, without any physician involvement. This takes place in an area entirely removed from the sick care sector, and in turn enables a three-way channeling of patients: toward sick care, the traditional modality; toward health self-care and education; or toward preventive maintenance. It would be useful to look at some diagrams in which Dr. Garfield, who is largely responsible for developing and continually modifying the Kaiser set-up, dramatizes in four basic shifts the changing nature of health care from the turn of the century.

Before 1900, health care was a simple, straight-line process for very sick people (see Figure 8). By 1935, the range of intervention had become much broader, adding those whom Garfield calls the early sick (see Figure 9).

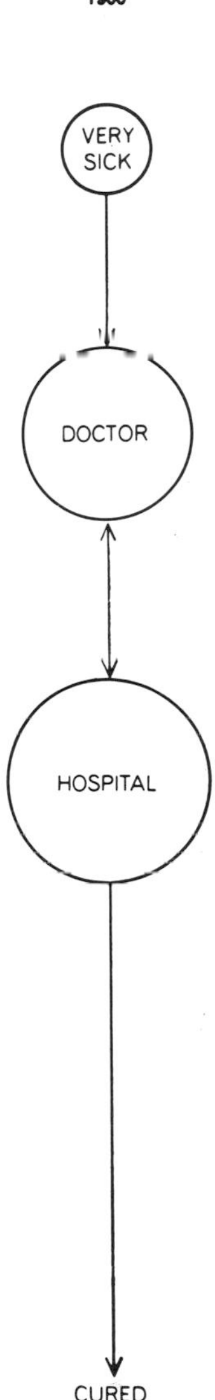

Fig. 8. *Traditional health care. [From "The Delivery of Medical Care," by Sidney R. Garfield, Copyright© by Scientific American, Inc. All rights reserved.]*

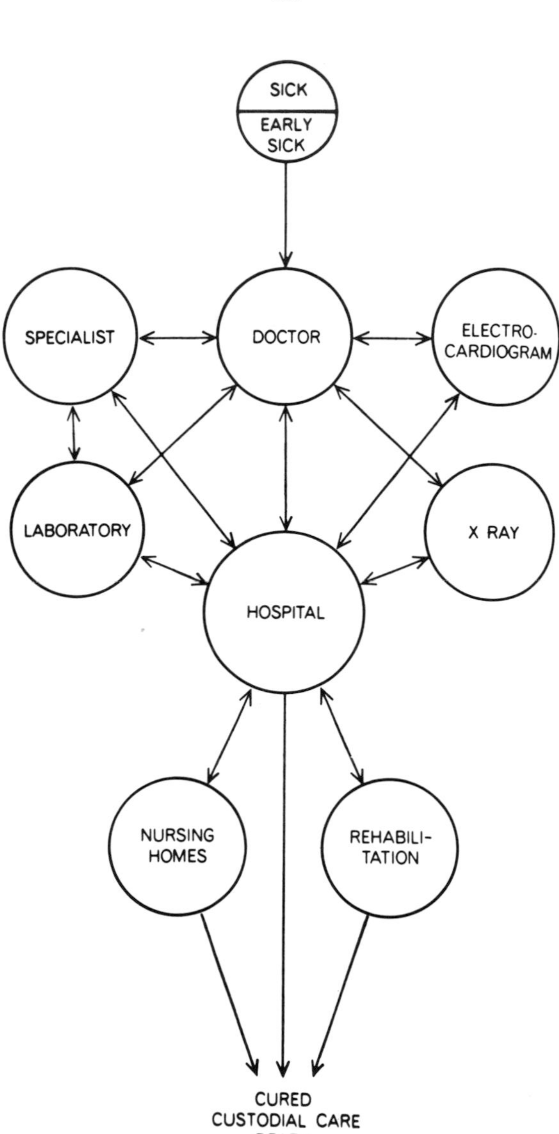

Fig. 9. *Health care in the 1930s. [From "The Delivery of Medical Care," by Sidney R. Garfield. Copyright© by Scientific American, Inc. All rights reserved.]*

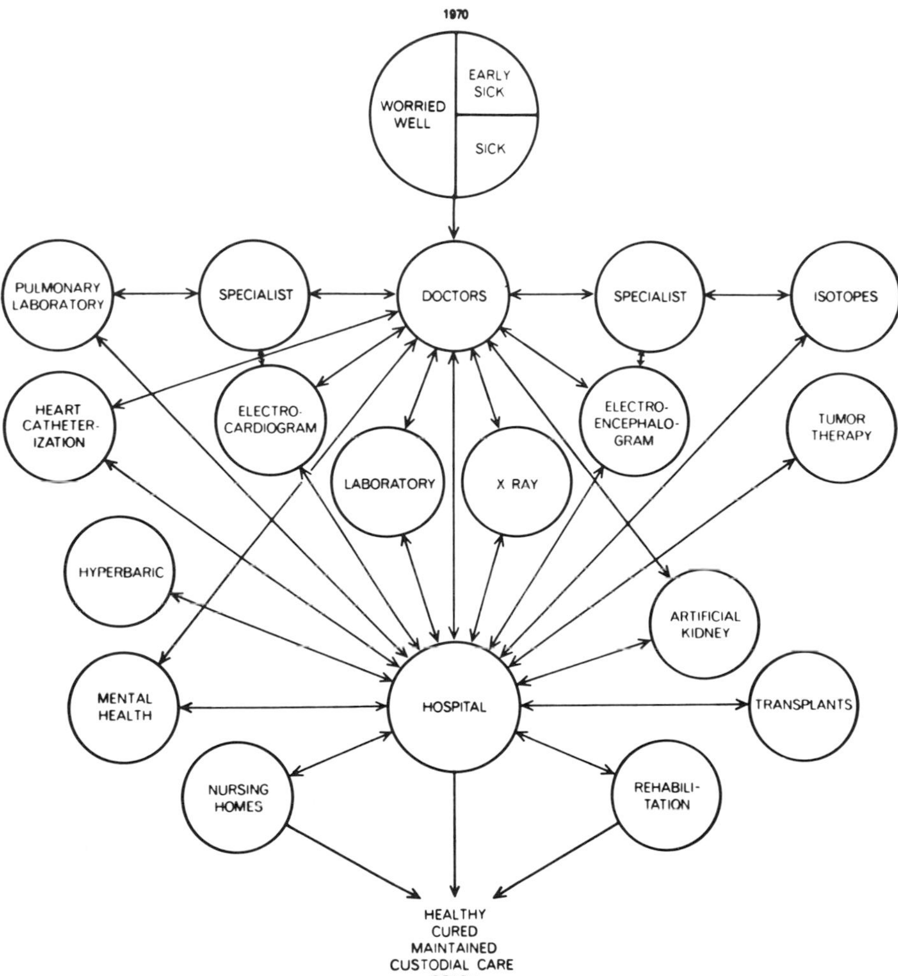

Fig. 10. *The present system. [From "The Delivery of Medical Care," by Sidney R. Garfield. Copyright© by Scientific American, Inc. All rights reserved.]*

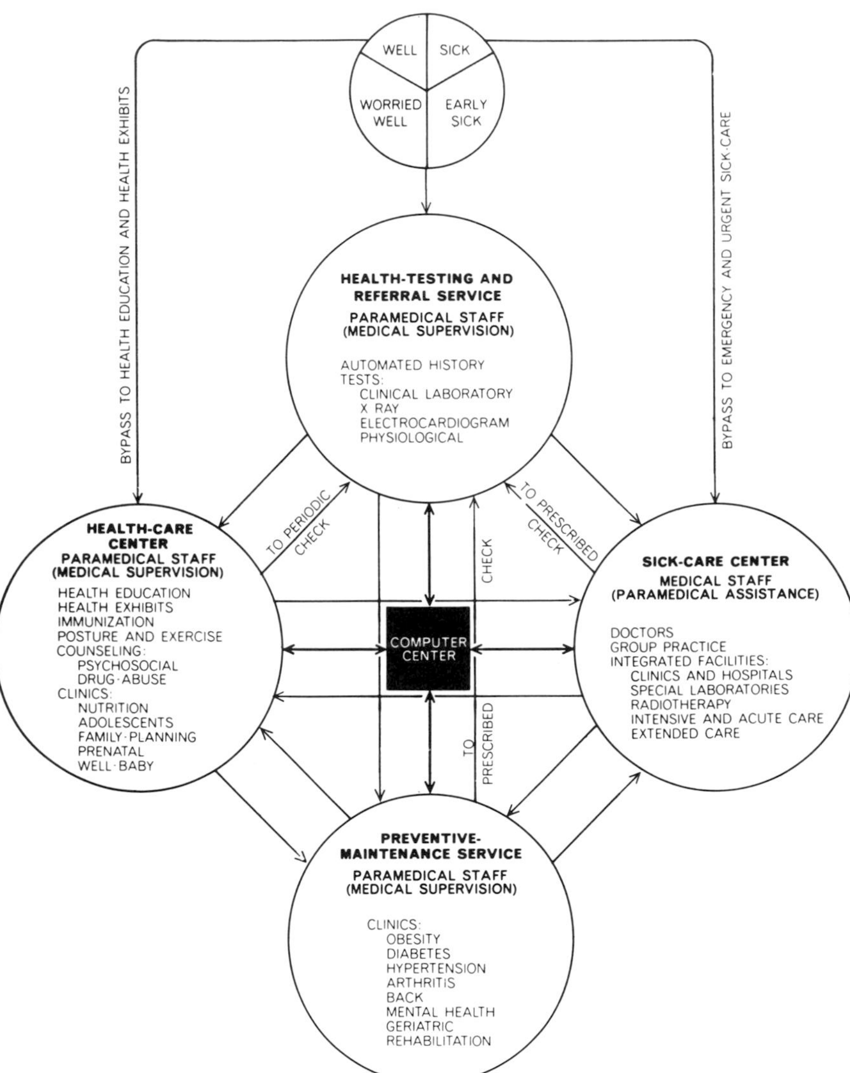

Fig. 11. *Dr. Garfield's new delivery system. [From "The Delivery of Medical Care," by Sidney R. Garfield. Copyright© by Scientific American, Inc. All rights reserved.]*

Ancillary treatment services, as well as rehabilitation programs and the ubiquitous nursing home, appear. After World War II, the explosion of medical technology, combined with greater utilization of health care facilities as a result of third-party payment, brings us to today's incredibly complex hospital-centered care (see Figure 10). Finally, there is a complete restructuring based in the first instance on health maintenance, with sick care now only one of four alternative channels (see Figure 11). While the Kaiser system is only one model, it illustrates the essential components of a future health care system which will require entirely new facility concepts and will radically modify the areas currently involving billions of dollars of investment.

Impact on Facility Design

The final consideration of this chapter is the facility environments required to match the proposed changes in the health care system.

1. Aside from continuing the hospital in modified form, the new facility environments will serve decentralized modalities of care housed in essentially small-scale, less complex settings. In time these units, instead of the hospital, may in fact become the heart of health care delivery.

2. They must be highly adaptive to a diversity of system needs and will take a wide range of forms, related both to their specific processing function and to the character of the community in which they are placed.

3. The new facility environments may emphasize conversion of existing nonmedical structures as much as, or more than, design of new overt facilities. Aside from cost economies, such reuse may increase psychological accessibility through greater familiarity and nondisruption of the community fabric.

4. The small-scale care facility is less likely to involve the large expenditures and commitments of capital outlays for major facility construction, and instead tend toward tenancy with its ease of locational shifts.

5. Smaller scale and a goal of maximum accessibility and acceptability, will tend to imbed the new facility environments as part of larger community activity focuses in joint occupancy settings such as shopping centers, multiservice centers, schools, housing, recreational, or transportation nodes. An example is the family and school clinic planned as part of the new Quincy School complex in Boston.

6. These environments will be less dependent on transportation for access, at least in urban areas, as they will be part of a network related whereever possible to pedestrian distances, as well as being electronically linked to distant medical services.

7. They will be maximally responsive to change through such factors as low investment (disposability) or demountability, internal modularity, and interchangeability of systems elements at low cost, mobility, reliance on movable equipment, and off-site electronic resources. Thus, the tendency of activities to become slaves of the rigid facilities which dominate them can be reversed, thereby eliminating one of the main causes of rapid obsolescence.

8. The new facility environment should be able to reduce institutionalization to a minimum and maximize psychologically supportive characteristics in the environment, with strong health educational inputs.

9. They must be developed as an outgrowth of a participatory process with the consumer community to make them truly effective environments: the consumers' territory and *their* health care are as integral parts of their lives as their homes.

10. Whether dispersed or at a centralized facility, the health care units must be so designed as to provide decentralized educational settings not only for medical students in a reoriented curriculum, but also for training of new, supportive categories of auxiliary health team personnel. This is a new area of investigation, cutting across many disciplines. It is not at all clear how the educational process will be locked into the non-hospital-based modalities and what impact this will have on the nature of facilities for these.

11. The facilities must provide for an integral research capacity within the care context, concerned as much with social and behavioral aspects of health, as with traditional concerns of biomedicine and pathology.

12. Finally there are the environmental impacts of these directives on the hospital itself. While not now available, a much deeper analysis of the exact nature of its processing systems is imperative. Successively, some of these will be uncoupled and become elements of a decentralized network. This will apply especially to many of the services related to ambulatory patients and primary care, triage, diagnosis, self-care and extended care. Such uncluttering should enable the hospital to reconstitute itself around the intensive application of skills, hardware, laboratory, and research capabilities relating to overt sickness and its treatment. A precondition would be an end to unplanned isolation and its replacement as a functioning part of integrated health care networks. Balanced and easy regional access within the network will be of prime importance in terms of transportation facilities and must become a prime locational determinant.

In the area of design, a great deal of effort should go to into measures countervailing the dehumanizing effects of a system geared to maximum process efficiency and automated surrogates instead of personal contact. There is no reason why oppressive hospital scales can not be broken down into "mini-hospital" communities within the same facility envelope, entities to which the patient can relate, individually and socially, for support. By moving much of the clutter of less specialized care activity out of the hospital, it should be easier to cope with such "humanizing," even in the face of the categorical priority of life saving and supportive measures. At the same time, there should be a continuous search for means that will permit greater indeterminateness in the design of hospitals, and for a nondisruptive, economical process of continuous self-renewal. If distant care and diagnosis become an important network component, the hospital is likely to be the central point, or origin, and will thus require specific new activity and equipment areas. While the patient environment is of focal concern, it should not be forgotten that the hospital is also a place of work. At present in the United States, some 3 million persons are employed in this setting. Their degree of satisfaction or disenchantment with their surroundings becomes, in turn, a parameter of the quality of the care itself.

Facility Types

While it is too early to pinpoint actual facility types likely to develop, some obvious examples which, in modified form, will probably be part of a future laundry list for the health care planner and designer are offered here. A definable entity is likely to develop in various models around the concept of preventive maintenance clinics, mainly in the form of community health centers. These health maintenance organizations could be independent, free-standing facilities, placed at a focal access point of the catchment area. Alternately, they could share occupancy as part of a multiservice center, a school, a housing project, a residential neighborhood, or a shopping center.

Considerable experimentation has taken place with various models in the NIMH Community Mental Health Centers Program. Another recent exploratory development is represented by the very varied clinics in urban and rural poverty areas sponsored by the Office of Economic Opportunity. One of the earliest of these in an urban setting is Boston's Columbia Point Clinic, initiated by the Tufts Medical School and set up in a wing of a 1500-unit public housing project. The Watts Clinic in Los Angeles provides an entirely separate center built of prefabricated system components, as does the rural health center in Mississippi's Bolivar County. Over several decades, Sweden and England have produced distinctive solutions, especially in new communities. The health care plan of the new city, Milton Keynes, in England shows a fully developed hierarchy of facility components.

Another entity may bring together uncoordinated bits of the present system now housed in completely inappropriate settings, or falling between the cracks altogether. For example, the handicapped, requiring adaptive living space either permanently or only during rehabilitation, constitute one of the categories most neglected and discriminated against. This neglect has resulted in the breakup of family life and the disappearance of otherwise healthy individuals into the destructive world of the nursing home. There is a range of related needs that might well produce a new mix of residential and semi-care facilities, allowing easy movement related to the degree of supportive requirements. Certainly some convalescent care, extended care, and self-care might, with appropriately designed settings, fit into such a grouping.

And certainly the American public will not forever tolerate the outrage of the so-called "nursing home." However, before the design aspects can be tackled to provide a benign environmental setting, a rethinking of the problem of chronic and terminal care in our society will have to take place—including the ethics of dying. At present, neither the financing mechanisms, nor the modality of care exists whereby new facility environments in these related areas may be brought together.

I would like to touch upon two more examples representing much more compressed settings. One is the mobile health unit—road, water, or air based. A very familiar, early model is the tuberculosis screening unit on wheels. With the tremendous and continuous advances in miniaturization and electronic aids, considerable treatment and diagnostic capability can be introduced into such a modality. It could also come into play as the kind of facility described by Dr. Garfield as a fourth element in his model, i.e., the health education and counseling unit, including immunization, family planning, routine obstetrics, and nutrition. Through its mobility, it could make the most continuous use of its manpower and equipment investment and bring such services as close as possible to home or workplace. In nonurban, sparsely populated areas the mobile health unit might become the main resource for all non-hospital-based services. In relation to emergency care, the use of the helicopter, or air ambulance, has tremendous potential. To date this has been exploited almost entirely as an adjunct to human salvage in military violence such as the American assault on Indochina. The air ambulance could also bring a range of services directly to relatively inaccessible localities, including those urban areas temporarily isolated through traffic congestion.

In some ways related to mobile possibilities, and in certain situations combined with them, is the video care and computer terminal unit. The on-site patient and nurse, or other auxiliary personnel, are hitched through audio-computer and television two-way communication to a physician at his place of work. Emergency measures, simple treatment, and diagnosis are already being handled successfully in this way. At Boston's Logan Airport, an experimental model has been functioning for over a year with considerable success. It is connected directly to the Massachusetts General Hospital Complex in downtown Boston, some two miles away. Staffed by a nurse, and other auxiliary help when needed, the unit is able to respond quickly to sickness episodes of arriving and departing passengers, visitors, or employees of the various airport facilities. In the absence of this video unit, the only recourse would be to have a physician available on site 24 hours a day, or to take the risk of moving acutely ill people through jammed-up roadways. Of course, the video care and computer terminal unit is now only a small, pilot venture, but it could be an infinitely expanded resource.

In facility expenditures, such a unit would involve very low investments of interior space and could be plugged into almost any setting. In fact, with further miniaturization and portability, it could become a means of bringing aspects of care back into the home setting—including the physician, this time not with his little black bag, but with the instant plug-in of major hospital resources. The visiting nurse or other auxiliaries, now offering mainly palliative support, could instantly provide the services of the health care team, including the input of the physician heading the team. Interestingly enough, the concept of nonfacility health care is almost realized here. New channels of low-cost care during disability, which provide partial alternatives to traditional hospitalization, are thus opened up.

In concluding this discussion of the interface of the changing health care system and its environment, I should emphasize two final aspects. First, the planning and design professions must break out of the traditional narrowness of their methodologies and concepts, which are simplistic in comparison with the complex factors involved in such problem solving and its resultant facilities. There must be greater inputs from a wide range of disciplines, coupled with greatly improved feedback mechanisms. Especially in the behavioral implications of planning and design a virtual vacuum exists. Knowledge of these implications is essential for effective evaluation of the architect's design. Design professionals, and especially architects, must overcome their passion to think in terms of buildings, and monumental ones at that. They must come back to a sense of human intimacy in their creativeness. This cannot be achieved if they continue to disparage remodeling and to treat interior space only as a second class concern.

Second, in relation to the anticipated colossal health care expenditures in financial, human, and other resources, there is a degree of absurdity in the minimal levels and quality of research back-up for the kinds of environmental settings provided. The unprecedented changes and their impact on facility concepts require a body of innovative thinking, as does the hospital in transition: Little of this is in sight. At most, there is a lot of fadism, gadgetry, and public relations disguised as research. A real methodology of research in facilities planning and design is lacking, as well as the critical use of evaluation. Unfortunately, too, whatever is done in other disciplines bearing on these aspects usually proves untranslatable.

A ray of hope is the move toward the establishment of a public funding corporation in health facilities research. A team consisting of William F. Maloney, Tufts University School of Medicine; Jerome Pollack, Harvard Medical School; and the author has been working on a study and recommendations for the funding of this corporation. Its financial support would come from a partnership of private foundations, government, industry, and the professions concerned. Among the major research areas considered especially urgent for such funding are:

1. development of suitable environments and facilities for health care systems
2. planning and design methodology
3. evaluation and evaluation techniques
4. financing of health care facilities
5. behavioral implications of designed environments
6. the community as client and consumer participant

Such research would be sponsored within a continually reevaluated strategy of priorities, and with the assurance of an adequate informational base, including inputs from abroad where significant work is being done—England and Sweden, for example. If and when this funding agency comes to pass, I hope that the professional participants and contracting teams will include strong representation of the behavioral and cognitive skills.

Perhaps the brief review of design implications of a radically changing health care system has produced more questions than answers. This is an exact reflection of 10 years of search at the Tufts–New England Medical Center, which in 1961, seemed to have much more certainty than in 1965 or 1970. Perhaps there is both a minus and a plus in all this: The minus is that continuing nonsolution of our basic societal crises is creating ever bigger disparities which threaten rational methodology; the plus is that professional rigidities are breaking down and, for the first time, the true complexity of the problems to be solved is recognized.

Chapter vi

Experimental Studies of Environment Perception

JOEL KAMERON
ENVIRONMENTAL PSYCHOLOGY PROGRAM
GRADUATE CENTER
CITY UNIVERSITY OF NEW YORK

In Chapter I some of the more general trends in contemporary psychology converging on the recognition of the importance of environment perception as a field of study were discussed. This led into an analysis of the issues which arise when the large-scale environment is considered the independent variable in perception—when the environment itself becomes the object of perception. This chapter will summarize the major studies, primarily of the past decade, which have addressed themselves experimentally to this question. It is not surprising, in light of the previous discussion, that the overwhelming majority of the more than 100 titles discussed here were not written by psychologists. Instead, they stem from a wide variety of other disciplines, including not only some of the behavioral sciences, but also geography, architecture, planning, and other branches of the design professions. This is no more than confirming evidence for the statement that environment perception has not been a subject of particularly active interest among psychologists.

It may be desirable to list what types of psychological investigations of perception have been omitted and to present the rationale for such omissions. The most obvious absentee is all of the vast literature devoted to space perception. As we have already seen, space perception is perhaps a misnomer, and the preponderance of work under this heading consists more of studies of the perception of objects in space, than of space itself. Indeed the introduction of the term "environment perception" is necessitated by the preemption of the term "space perception" for an area of study which deals with basically quite different subject matter. In addition to the literature on space perception, most of the classical and basic psychological studies of object perception have also been omitted from this review. This is, of course, dictated by the definition of the subject of the review as environment perception, rather than object perception. Nevertheless, it remains true that the major generalizations presumably relating to environment perception which are to be found in psychological literature grow out of studies of object perception; and the task of comparing the conclusions from studies of environment perception with those from object perception remains before us.

Also excluded from this review is a large body of studies which do deal explicitly with the large-scale environment. The reason for this is more one of economy of space and the availability of reviews elsewhere, than of any inappropriateness of the material itself. Broadly speaking, this class of studies can be described as the effect of environmental experience on perceptual processes, both object and environment perception. In this context the reader will immediately think of classical studies such as those involving inversion lenses and other types of distorting lenses; relating specific kinds of environmental experiences to perception; and cultural and cross-cultural studies (such as Allport & Pettigrew, 1957; Antonovsky & Ghent, 1964; Deregowski, 1968; Hallowell, 1957). This wide range of studies concerning perceptual adaptation and perceptual learning is excellently reviewed elsewhere (Epstein, 1967; Rock, 1966; Segall, Campbell, & Herskovits, 1966).

As has already been suggested, the motivation for much of the work reported in this chapter came from the need of architects, planners, and resource managers to understand the perceptual processes of their clients—a need reflected in the work of Izumi (1967) and Osmond (1957). The growing interest in environmental problems in recent years has underscored the need, already expressed by designers, for an understanding of the perception of complex environmental situations—ranging from rooms, to buildings, to entire cities, and natural environments. With very few exceptions, this has led to studies in existing real-world environments; and attempts at laboratory investigations have been extremely limited. The application of this research to the design process and to resource management has already begun; but the need for further research is pressing.

Studies of the perception of complex environments have been undertaken in a wide variety of settings. The discussion here will be devoted to four environmental classifications: architectural forms; cities; highways and streets; and natural settings. Relatively few works are devoted to the broader considerations of environmental perception in general which transcend the particular setting, or at least encompass a variety of settings. In the most comprehensive discussion of this kind, Craik (1968a) outlined the range of research paradigms that are applicable to the study of everyday physical environments and listed alternatives for each of four different research elements. As observers, he suggested special competence groups (e.g., architects), special user groups (e.g., the elderly), and groups formed on the basis of personality measures. As displays, he considered the use of varying modes of direct experiences, as well as a number of simulation techniques. In addition, he reviewed the major psychological assessment devices, such as adjective checklists, TAT analysis, ratings, and *Q* sorts (see also Craik, 1969); and also considered validation criteria.

Lowenthal (1967a,b, 1971) addressed some of these issues more directly with both empirical research and general discussion; while Saarinen (1969) provided a broad framework for considering all kinds of environments, from room to planetary scale. Ittelson (1970) and Nahemow (1971) reported research in a novel laboratory environment, designed to assess how man perceives variations and structure within his environment. Observers' descriptions of the environment were categorized as either structural—in which the environment was described in objective terms; or experiential—which included the feelings and impressions of the observer himself in his description of the environment. The latter group was more likely to report enjoyment of the environment.

In another vein, many writers addressing themselves to research applications have urged that the study of the perception of complex environments be applied to a variety of design problems. Kates (1966) and Brower (1965) emphasized the symbolic information that environments transmit, and the need to consider this in environmental design. Parr (1963) suggested that simulation techniques be used to assess man's response to radically altered environments before they are actually built. In contrast to these relatively few works dealing with environment perception in general terms, the majority of reports dealt with the study of specific environmental contexts.

Architectural Forms

Architects, architectural critics, and art historians have written extensively about how people perceive architectural structures. The rich and fascinating literature on this topic, which reveals the insights and judgments of some of the great minds, will not be mentioned, for it has been reviewed in many works on architectural history. A quite different consideration, however, is suggested by studies (Canter, 1961, 1969; Hershberger, 1968; Payne, 1969) indicating that architects perceive the world in ways quite different from those of the general public. The lack of congruence between the perceptions of the designer (as reflected in his design) and those of the user group for whom the design was intended is illustrated in several studies (Environmental Research Foundation, 1968; Izumi, 1957; Osmond, 1961, 1966) which deal with the psychiatric facility. "Learning from Las Vegas," by Venturi, Brown, and Izenour (Chapter IV) and the introductory comments by Ittelson further highlight the necessity of distinguishing between expert and user viewpoints. Thus, the purpose of this survey can better be served by examining empirical studies which deal with the perceptions of people who are more representative of the population as a whole.

As a starting point in this field, Rasmussen (1959), in *Experiencing Architecture*, covered many of the basic ideas. Halldane (1968b) reported on complex psychophysical research designed to discover any existing "S–R" relationships in architectural perception, and proposed (Halldane, 1968a) that research of this type be eventually used to ensure that designs reflect their designers' intentions. Similar research also was done by Burnham and Grimm (1970); they attempted to measure the psychological meanings of surfaces which have to match with the overall meanings of the design concept. In this respect, they are approaching another area of research, that of "meaning" in architecture in general, which can only be briefly mentioned here.

Wohlwill (1966) was an early proponent of the application of this type of research to the design process; Beck (1967) also discussed it. A thorough discussion of this topic is found in Hesselgren's book (1967), *The Language of Architecture,* which includes sections on basic and holistic perceptual processes. Collins (1968) limited his research on architectural meaning to the verbal dimensions of architectural space. Using a factor analysis of descriptive nouns, he found eight dimensions: disorderly, cheerful, dramatic, big, active, familiar, jagged, and festive. Similarly, Sanoff (1968) has described work on a semantic differential scale for environmental description. A factor analysis of his results yielded three factors: factor one described the associated components of preferred environments; factor two, perceptually anonymous environments; and factor three, redundant environments. Hershberger (1968) has attempted to determine the presence of a code used by architects to communicate meaning to the public in the physical attributes of buildings. He had four groups of subjects rate 25 building aspects on 30 semantic scales; differences between the ratings of the architects and the public were found.

The room is one of the basic units of architectural design; and a proportionate amount of research has been devoted to its study. Maslow and Mintz (1956), for example, investigated the psychological effects of exposure to "beautiful" and "ugly" rooms. Subjects rated photographs of faces on two dimensions, fatigue–energy and displeasure–well-being, presented in each of three rooms: "beautiful," "ugly," and "average." In the beautiful room, the faces were rated as more well-being and energetic. In a similar study in which patients rated a psychiatric interviewer, Kasmar, Griffin, and Mauritzen (1968) were unable to show clear effects of room quality on the perceptions of the interviewers. Birren (1961), perhaps on a more basic level, considered the effects of color on the basic physiological and psychological state of the person. Spivak (1967) reported that psychotics are more prone to the distortions caused by long corridors than are scientists. Others (Holmberg, Almgren, Söderpalm, & Küller, 1967; Holmberg, Küller, & Tidblom, 1966) have investigated the relationship between the ratio of length, width, and height, and the perception of room volume. Finally, Kasmar (1965, 1970) has developed a semantic scale for the description of the environment and more specifically, of rooms. Her 66 bipolar scales differentiated between three rooms, but were stable over time in the same room.

Canter and Wools (1969) have developed reliable techniques for appraising buildings. They used three semantic differential scales: one concerning how inspiring a building was; another, its harmony; and the third, its friendliness. These scales were applied to a number of different rooms and houses; and were able to meaningfully discriminate between them—as well as between individually arranged differences in elements (i.e., seating arrangements). The scales also differentiated people in terms of their sensitivity to the environment. In a related study, Canter (1969) showed that architectural and nonarchitectural students differed in their ratings of plans and elevations. Results of factor analysis indicated that three factors—friendliness, coherence, and character—were important in architects' ratings; only the first two factors, in nonarchitects' ratings. Collins (1970) related semantic differential descriptions of three libraries to behavioral criteria (how they were actually used) and found correlations in the range .33–.50.

Much research has dealt with the exterior quality of housing and its perception. Peterson, Bishop, and Fitzgerald (1969) studied housing preferences and found that they depended mainly on sound physical quality and harmony with nature, and, to a lesser degree, on variety and richness. Specifically, where X_1 is physical quality rating, X_2 is harmony with nature rating, and X_3 is variety and richness, preference is equal to

$.72X_1 + .60X_2 + .26X_3$. Goodman (1968) showed that windshield surveys of housing quality by urban renewal specialists were prone to a number of possible biasing factors, such as the condition of adjacent structures or excessively "gingerbread" design. Chermayeff and Alexander (1963) discussed the relationship of housing design to real and perceived privacy.

Site plan also affects the perceptual display impinging on the viewer. A thorough discussion of the effect of various design elements on site perception is given by Lynch (1962) in his book, *Site Planning.* The chapter on "Visual Form" is especially relevant. Among the empirical research in this area is the work of Downs (1970) who studied the mental image of an urban shopping center. Using a set of 36 semantic differential scales as the operational definition of the image, he found that it was eight-dimensional. Weiss and Boutourline (1962) studied various world fair exhibits and included such factors as the way in which the perceptual properties of entrances and exits influenced crowd flow. Newman (1969) discussed the effect of the site plan of a public housing project on perceived "defensibility" of the area by tenants. He suggested that certain groupings of buildings and certain entrance designs led tenants to perceive the lobbies and yards as part of their territory, and hence as defensible.

Perception of Cities

Urban planners and designers are concerned with the manner in which the products of their efforts are perceived by the public. What elements of the design are most salient to the perceiver? What are his preferences—complexity or simplicity, old or new, variety or redundancy? Many of these questions have been researched and some answers are beginning to emerge.

A number of general articles are concerned with the perception of cities from a subjective viewpoint. For example, Lynch (1965) has discussed the city as an environment for man and noted its shortcomings. An excellent summary by Lynch (1954) dealt with elements such as size, grain (functional differentiation), density, shape, and internal pattern which determine the form of cities. Strauss (1968) also discussed the visual appearances of American cities. He stated that cities have personalities based on their histories, as well as their physical forms. An interesting photographic essay on environments, and particularly on American cities, is that of Swinburne (1967); in it he noted that what we see depends, to an extent, on our values and attitudes. Value systems associated with visual environments have been examined by Van der Ryn and Boie (1963). Carp (1968) studied the implications of environmental change in terms of past experience and expectations of the elderly. A number of writers have urged that urban designs reflect the needs of the public. Among them, Wohlwill (1966) and Rappaport and Hawkes (1970) emphasized the need for complexity and variety; Steinitz (1968) urged that form enhance, rather than inhibit, activity and achievement. Field (Chapter V) discussed the need to "humanize" health care facilities in the face of increasing mechanization.

Another related area of research is the measurement of urban preferences. Michelson (1966) investigated urban preferences by intensively interviewing 75 residents. He stressed that planners should reduce the physical environment to its most basic level, the view of the individual (see also Michelson, 1968a,b). In researching urban perception, Lowenthal (1968a) has concluded that: people prefer environments about whose character they disagree; men and women disagree in their attitudes toward spatial density; and preconceptions and stereotypes govern many responses to the environment. Southworth (1969) has studied the "sonic environment of cities" and its relationship to the visual forms of the city. Preferred sound settings were responsive, nonrepetitive, and in the middle range of frequency and intensity. Lansing and Marans (1969), and Webber and Webber (1967) both emphasized the necessity for user need and preference research. They stressed the need to avoid making decisions based entirely on the input of the elite. The study of "mental maps" and "urban images" has been one of the major areas of interest in urban perception. Here, the concern is with the maps or pictures of the city that people have in their minds; how they develop; what affects their form; how the maps differ from individual to individual; and how they influence behavior. Chapter II of this volume (Saarinen) on the mental maps of a university and of the entire world represents the range of this line of research.

A classic study on mental maps was Lynch's (1960) *The Image of the City*. Choosing to measure the "public image" and to ignore individual differences, Lynch showed that the "imageability" of the city is determined mainly by certain elements including paths, edges, nodes, districts, and landmarks. He argued that highly imageable cities are desired both on esthetic and pragmatic grounds. Carr (1966) basically agreed with this viewpoint, but argued that there would be great individual differences in the images and the needs of the citizens, based on the relative social value that particular districts have for them. Stea (1969b) has also done extensive research on mental maps, concluding that people order their conceptions of the environment in terms of hierarchies, bounds, locations, relationships between points, and connectedness (paths). Good reviews of the history of mental mapping have also been written (Blaut & Stea, 1969; Downs & Stea, 1971; Stea, 1969a; Stea & Downs, 1970).

The psychological effects of city form are discussed by Alexander (1969). He proposed 20 new form patterns based on the conceptions of human needs put forth by three psychological theorists (Leighton, Maslow, and Erikson). Milgram (1970) has also discussed the effects of urban images on the inhabitants of modern cities. He included a study of the recognition value of New York City and found that most inhabitants recognized only a limited section of the midtown area.

Many writers have been concerned with the elements which comprise the mental map. Lynch's (1960) results have previously been mentioned; other writers have extended and modified his list. Stea (1969b) has found that maps are affected by several factors, including attractiveness, familiarity, scale being considered, barriers, and frequently used routes. Furthermore, he reported research dealing with increasing scales, from short distances to the global scale. Many studies of specific urban areas have confirmed that inputs other than physical form contribute to the imageability of an area. For example, Gulick (1963) showed that sociocultural associations influenced the predominance of some physically nondistinct areas in mental maps of inhabitants of certain Arab cities. DeJonge (1962) verified many of Lynch's findings for several cities in the Netherlands. However, he also showed that when characteristic nodes, landmarks, and the like were not available, greater attention was paid to individual details. Ekman and Bratfisch (1965) demonstrated that in Sweden the subjective distance to cities was inversely proportional to the emotional involvement in the city. Lee (1970) has shown that values and satisfactions associated with the downtown foreshorten the perceived distance in that direction, as opposed to perceived distance to locations away from the downtown. Wastlund and Wihervuori (1962) have shown that action contributed to high imageability of areas in Stockholm. Firey (1945) has discussed the role of sentiment and symbolism as ecological variables which affect the mental image. Finally, Passonneau (1965) has written on the temporal aspect of the urban image. He stated that the city is the unity of both temporal and spatial dimensions within the image we have of that city.

Another area of interest is the effect of observer variables on the nature of the urban image. Carr (1966) emphasized the roles of individual needs and values as determinants of the form of the mental image. Appleyard (1970) dealt with the effects of age, sex, occupation, and familiarity on the mental maps of the residents of Ciudad, Guayana. He urged that "visibility" be a consideration in urban design in order to facilitate residents' use of available services. Ladd (1970) studied the neighborhood maps of black youths and, unlike Appleyard, found little or no relationship between "map groups" and age, grade levels, or length of residence. Age, however, was considered a critical variable by Blaut, McCleary, and Blaut (1970) who investigated the developmental aspects of mental mapping. They found that preliterate children could perform a relatively complex set of mapping tasks. This was further amplified by Blaut and Stea (1970). They have also considered factors such as enrichment and experience as they affect spatial learning in children; and the implications for environmental design (Stea & Blaut, 1970).

Perception of Highways and Streets

Much of our lives is spent on highways or on sidewalks next to streets. Thus, the question of how we perceive and react to streets is not trivial. Appleyard, Lynch, and Meyer (1964) advocated that an automobile passenger's view of the city as he speeds along an expressway should: contribute meaningfully to the "imageability" of the city; give the viewer a rich, coherent, visual form; and deepen his grasp of the meaning of the environment. This, of course, has implications for the placement of expressways. Carr and Schissler (1969) found a significant correlation between what was looked at on a trip and what was remembered after it was over. They found that the actual physical structure of the roadside vistas strongly influenced the results.

The role of individual differences in response to the roadside environment is considered by Little (1968) and Winkel, Malek, and Thiel (1969). Results of factor analysis indicated the importance of three attitudes in an individual's response to the roadside environment: a negative sentiment concerning urban roadside; a preference for simplicity, order, and good taste; and an emphasis on expression of action and vitality. Golledge and Zannaras (Chapter III of this volume) examined individual differences in the perception of optimum route. The most thoroughgoing study of the perception of city streets was done by Appleyard and Lintell (1970) who measured residents' perceptions of high, medium, and low traffic streets. Amount of traffic affected the perception of noise, danger, and dirt; and low traffic streets were viewed more as recreation areas and as gathering places. Other studied indirectly involving city streets are by Vigier (1965) in which doubt is cast on the strength of traditional architectural elements, and by Lynch and Rivkin (1959) who studied people's reactions as they circled a block in Boston.

Perception of Natural Environments

Most of the preceding discussion has been concerned with man-made or man-influenced environments. One could argue, along ecological lines, that there are few, if any, truly "natural" areas remaining in the world. Be that as it may, areas are often perceived which are predominantly "natural" in make-up. Studies and theories of the perception of natural areas are thus vital to an understanding of environmental perception in general.

One broad area of interest could be termed "geographic perception." This concerns the way in which individuals perceive the world, i.e., how they form their world view. Columbus' notion that he had landed in the East Indies is an example of a misperception based on an inaccurate world view. Sprout and Sprout (1965) discussed the nonveridical nature of perception within the context of world view. Lowenthal (1967c) distinguished between consensual and personal world views–emphasizing the role of past experience, cultural forces, and feelings as determinants. Campbell (1968) discussed the role of personality and perception as its affects the geographer's conceptualization of region. The general conclusion of research of this type is that a person's world view is a result of "the real world" and his attitudes, beliefs, and experiences.

The other major direction of research in this area concerns the perception of natural environments on a smaller scale. Shafer (1969) reviewed research and theories of natural environment perception, and also reported his own studies on subjects' perceptions of campsites. He stressed the role of individual needs and values in determining preferences for certain types of campsites. Craik (1968b) has proposed a research paradigm for the study of human responsiveness to landscape. It takes into consideration mode of presentation, response format, observer characteristics, and description of the environment used. Lowenthal (1966, 1968b) also discussed Americans' attitudes and perceptions of landscape and their values concerning it.

Specific research on natural environments has been done by Sonnenfeld (1969). He hypothesizes that populations occupying different environments will not differ in their perception of contextual elements of their environments, but will differ in their perception of focal elements. Data from Delaware and Alaska have generally supported these predictions. However, personality variables have been implicated as a possible source of "within population" differences. Sonnenfeld (1967) has also compared several distinctive populations in their preferences for relief, vegetation, water, and temperature.

Related research has been done in the area of hazard perception. Saarinen (1966) has studied drought perception on the Great Plains, and Kates (1962) has studied the perception of flood hazards. Both concluded that the role of past experience with hazards and the relative likelihood of their occurrence influenced the residents' perceptions of them. Burton (1970) proposed research to evaluate the role of cultural and personality variables. Sewell (1970) has shown that engineers tended to perceive water pollution as an economic problem; whereas public health officials perceived it as a health problem. Craik (1970) has provided an excellent summary of this work on hazard perception in his article, *Environmental Psychology.*

The range of studies reviewed in this chapter is vast; and yet, it is clear that many questions remain to be answered. This is due to a number of factors. First, the bulk of the research has been done by people in diverse fields. Thus, while often well executed, it was not designed to aid in the development of a general model of environment perception. Instead, its purpose was to aid architects and planners in elucidating and solving relatively specific design problems. While this is certainly a valuable pursuit, more basic research remains to be done.

Second, the "stimulus–response" model employed in most of the cited research is inadequate. One assumption of this approach is that the "stimulus" is known. However, the task of conceptualizing the environment is yet to be completed. Thus, the ability to specify the "stimulus" is limited. In addition, precise methods of measuring environmental "response" are also undeveloped. Do we measure fantasy, attitude, behavior, or effect of behavior? The man–environment system is a complex network involving interaction and feedback, a complexity that is beyond the scope of the "*S–R*" model. Systems theory appears, at present, to be a more viable approach.

The research reviewed here has many strong points which should also be noted. Much of it was done in "naturalistic" settings, under relatively "normal" conditions. Such research is far more difficult to execute than that done in controlled, laboratory settings; moreover, there is a need for this type of research in the field of environment perception. Many different types of user groups served as subjects; thus, results tend to be representative of the population as a whole. Finally, several interesting and innovative experimental techniques were used; this represents a contribution to behavioral sciences in general.

References

Preface

Antrobus, J. S. (Ed.). *Cognition and affect.* Boston: Little, Brown, 1970.
Segal, S. J. *Imagery. Current cognitive approaches.* New York: Academic Press, 1971.
Singer, J. *The control of aggression and violence.* New York: Academic Press, 1970.

Chapter I

Environment Perception and Contemporary Perceptual Theory

Allport, G., & Pettigrew, T. Cultural influence on the perception of movement: The trapezoidal illusion among the Zulus. *Journal of Abnormal and Social Psychology,* 1957, **55**, 104-113.
Bridgman, P. W. Science and common sense. *Scientific Monthly,* 1954 (July), 32-39.
Bruner, J. S. Constructive cognitions. *Contemporary Psychology,* 1970, **15** (2), 81-83.
Brunswik, E. *Perception and the representative design of psychological experiments.* Berkeley: Univ. of California Press, 1956.
Cantril, H. (Ed.). *The morning notes of Adelbert Ames, Jr. (including a correspondence with John Dewey).* Rahway, New Jersey: Rutgers Univ. Press, 1960.
Chomsky, N. *Language and mind.* New York: Harcourt, 1968.
Dewey, J., & Bentley, A. F. *Knowing and the known.* Boston, Massachusetts: Beacon, 1949.
Gibson, J. J. *The perception of the visual world.* Boston, Massachusetts: Houghton, 1950.
Gibson, J. J. *The senses considered as perceptual systems.* Boston, Massachusetts: Houghton, 1966.
von Helmholtz, H. L. F. *Helmholtz's treatise on physiological optics.* Translated from the third German edition. J. P. C. Southall, (Ed.). New York: Dover, 1962.

von Helmholtz, H. L. F. The facts of perception. In R. M. Warren & R. P. Warren (Eds.), *Helmholtz on perception: Its physiology and development.* New York: Wiley, 1968.
Ittelson, W. H. *Visual space perception.* New York: Springer Publ., 1960.
Kiss, G. Memory forgotten? *Contemporary Psychology,* 1971, **16**(9), 609-610.
Neisser, U. The processes of vision. *Scientific American,* 1968, **219**(3), 204-214.
Rock, I. *The nature of perceptual adaptation.* New York: Basic Books, 1966.
Segall, M. H., Campbell, D. T., & Herskovits, M. J. *Influence of culture on visual perception.* Indianapolis: Bobbs-Merrill, 1966.
Stevens, S. S. *Handbook of experimental psychology.* New York: Wiley, 1966.
Tolman, E. C., & Brunswik, E. The organism and the causal texture of the environment. *Psychological Review,* 1935, **42**, 43-77.
Whitehead, A. N. *The aims of education, and other essays.* New York: Macmillan, 1957.
Wundt, W. *An introduction to psychology.* London: Allen & Unwin, 1912.

Chapter II

Introduction

Hooper, D. A pedestrian's view of New York, London and Paris. Unpublished manuscript, Harvard Univ., 1966. Cited by S. Milgram, The experience of living in cities. *Science,* 1970, **167**, P. 1468.
Huntington, E. *Mainsprings of civilization.* New York: Wiley, 1945.
Lynch, K. *The image of the city.* Cambridge, Massachusetts: M.I.T. & Harvard Univ. Press, 1960.
Turner, F. J. The significance of the frontier in American history. *Report of the American Historical Association,* 1893. Cited by F. J. Turner, Western state-making in the revolutionary era. *American Historical Review,* 1895, **1**, P. 71.

The Use of Projective Techniques in Geographic Research

Barker, M., & Burton, I. Differential response to stress in natural and social environments: An application of a modified Rosenzweig picture-frustration test. *Natural Hazard Research Working Paper.* Toronto: Natural Hazard Research, Univ. of Toronto, 1969, No. 5.
Boulding, K. E. National images and international systems. *Journal of Conflict Resolution,* 1959, **3**, 120-131. Also in R. E. Kasperson & J. V. Minghi (Eds.), *The structure of political geography.* Chicago: Aldine, 1969.
Burton, I., Kates, R. W., & White, G. F. The human ecology of extreme geophysical events. *Natural Hazard Research Working Paper.* Toronto: Natural Hazard Research, Univ. of Toronto, 1968, No. 1.
Cole, J. P. The Carioca's view of the world. *Ideas in Geography,* 1970, **26**.
Cox, K. R., & Zannaras, G. Designative perceptions of macro-spaces: Concepts, a methodology, and applications. *Department of Geography Discussion Paper,* Columbus Ohio: Ohio State Univ. Press, 1970, No. 17.
Gould, P. R. On mental maps. *Michigan Inter-University Community of Mathematical Geographers Discussion Paper,* Ann Arbor: Univ. of Michigan Press, 1966, No. 9.

Haddon, J. A view of foreign lands. *Geography,* 1960, **65**, 286-289.

Henry, W. E. Executive personality and job success. *Personnel Series.* New York: American Management Association, 1948, No. 120.

Henry, W. E. The business executive: The psychodynamics of a social role. *American Journal of Sociology,* 1949, **54**, 286-291.

Henry, W. E. *The analysis of fantasy: The thematic apperception technique in the study of personality.* New York: Wiley, 1956.

Kates, R. W. Hazard and choice perception in flood plain management. *Department of Geography Research Paper,* Chicago: Univ. of Chicago Press, 1964, No. 78.

Lindzey, G. *Projective techniques and cross-cultural research.* New York: Appleton, 1961.

Lindzey, G., & Thorpe, J. H. Projective techniques. In D. L. Sills (Ed.), *International encyclopedia of the social sciences.* Vol. 12. New York: Free Press, 1968.

Lynch, K. *The image of the city.* Cambridge, Massachusetts: M.I.T. & Harvard Univ. Press, 1960.

Metton, A. Le quartier: Etudes géographiques et psycho-sociologiques. *Canadian Geographer,* 1969, **13**, 299-316.

Murray, A. *Thematic apperception test: Pictures and manual.* Cambridge, Massachusetts: Harvard Univ. Press, 1943.

Murray, H. A. *Explorations in personality.* New York: Oxford Univ. Press, 1930. (Republished: New York; Science Editions, 1962.)

A New Yorker's idea of the United States of America. *The Saturday Review of Literature,* 1936, **55**(5), 4.

Robinson, J. P., & Hefner, R. Perceptual maps of the world. *Public Opinion Quarterly,* 1968, **32**, 273-280.

Russett, B. M. Discovering voting groups in the United Nations. *American Political Science Review,* 1966, **60**, 327-339. Also in R. E. Kasperson & J. V. Minghi (Eds.), *The structure of political geography.* Chicago: Aldine, 1969.

Saarinen, T. F. Perception of the drought hazard on the Great Plains. *Department of Geography Research Paper.* Chicago: Univ. of Chicago, 1966, No. 106.

Saarinen, T. F. Image of the University of Arizona campus. Unpublished manuscript, Univ. of Arizona, 1967.

Saarinen, T. F. Perception of environment. *Commission on College Geography Resource Paper.* Washington, D.C.: Association of American Geographers, 1969, No. 5.

Saarinen, T. F. Student views of the world. In R. M. Downs & D. Stea (Eds.), *Cognitive mapping: Images of spatial environment.* Chicago: Aldine, 1971.

Schaw, L. C., & Henry, W. E. A method for the comparison of groups: A study in thematic apperception. *Genetic Psychology Monographs,* 1956, **54**, 207-253.

Sims, J. N. Psychodynamics of two levels of executives in the federal civil service. Unpublished doctoral dissertation, Univ. of Chicago, 1964.

Sims, J., & Saarinen, T. F. Coping with environmental threat: Great Plains farmers and the sudden storm. *Annals of the Association of American Geographers,* 1969, **59**, 677-686.

Sprout, H., & Sprout, M. *The ecological perspective on human affairs.* Princeton, New Jersey: Princeton Univ. Press, 1965.

Steinbeck, J. *The grapes of wrath.* New York: Viking, 1939.

White, G. F. Choice of adjustment to floods. *Department of Geography Research Paper,* Chicago: Univ. of Chicago Press, 1964, No. 93.

White, G. F. Optimal flood damage management: Retrospect and prospect. In A. V. Knesse & S. C. Smith (Eds.), *Water research.* Baltimore, Maryland: Johns Hopkins Press, 1966.

Zannaras, G. An empirical analysis of urban neighborhood perception. Unpublished masters thesis, Ohio State Univ., 1968.

Chapter III

Introduction

Lynch, K. *The image of the city.* Cambridge, Massachusetts: M.I.T. & Harvard Univ. Press, 1960.

Orleans, P. Urban experimentation and urban sociology. In Science, engineering and the city. Symposium sponsored jointly by the National Academy of Sciences and the National Academy of Engineering. Washington, D.C.: National Academy of Sciences, 1967, No. 1498.

Cognitive Approaches to the Analysis of Human Spatial Behavior

Adams, J. S. Directional bias in intra-urban migration. *Economic Geography*, 1969, **45**, 302-323.

Appleyard, D., Lynch, K., & Meyer, J. R. *The view from the road.* Cambridge, Massachusetts: M.I.T. Press, 1964.

Berry, B. J. L. Interdependencies of spatial structure and spatial behavior. *Papers and Proceedings of the Regional Scienve Association,* 1968, **21**, 205-228.

Berry, B. J. L., Barnum, H., & Tennant, R. J. Retail location and consumer behavior. *Papers and Proceedings of the Regional Science Assocation*, 1962, **8**, 65-106.

Briggs, R. The scaling of preferences for spatial locations: An example using shopping centers. Unpublished masters thesis, Ohio State Univ., 1969.

Briggs, R. Urban cognitive distances. Unpublished doctoral dissertation, Ohio State Univ., 1971.

Brown, L., & Holmes, J. Intra-urban migrant lifelines: A spatial view. *Demography*, 1970, **8**, 103-122.

Brown, L. A., & Moore, E. G. The intra-urban migration process: A perspective. *Geografiska Annaler,* **52**, (Series B). Also in *Yearbook of the Journal Systems Society,* 1970, No. 15.

Carr, S., & Schissler, D. The city as trip. *Environment and Behavior,* 1969, **1**, 7-35.

Christaller, W. *Central places in southern Germany.* Translated by C. W. Baskin. Englewood Cliffs, New Jersey: Prentice-Hall, 1966.

Curry, L. Central places in the random spatial economy. *Journal of Regional Science,* 1967, **7** (Supplement).

Golledge, R. G. A conceptual framework of a market decision process. *Department of Geography Discussion Paper.* Univ. of Iowa, 1967, No. 4. (a)

Golledge, R. G. Conceptualizing the market decision process. *Journal of Regional Science,* 1967, **7**, 239-358. (b)

Golledge, R. G., Briggs, R., & Demko, D. The configuration of distances in intra-urban space. *Proceedings of the Association of American Geographers,* 1969, 60-66.

Golledge, R. G., & Brown, L. A. Search, learning and the market decision process. *Geografiska Annaler,* 1967, **49**(Series B), 116-124.

Golledge, R. G., Clark, W. A. V., & Rushton, G. The implications of the consumer behavior of a dispersed farm population in Iowa. *Economic Geography,* 1965, **41**.

Golledge, R. G., & Rushton, G. Multidimensional scaling: Review and geographical applications. Unpublished manuscript, 1970.

Golledge, R. G., & Zannaras, G. The perception of urban structure: An experimental approach. In J. Archea & C. Eastman (Eds.), *EDRA two. Proceedings of the second annual Environmental Design Research Association conference.* Pittsburgh, Pennsylvania: Carnegie Press, 1970.

Huff, D. A topological model of consumer space preferences. *Papers and Proceedings of the Regional Science Association,* 1962, **6**, 157-173.

Keller, S. *The urban neighborhood: A sociological perspective.* New York: Random House, 1968.

Lee, T. R. Psychology and living space. *Transactions of the Bartlett Society,* 1963-1964, 11-37.

Lee, T. R. Urban neighborhood as a socio-spatial schema. *Human Relations,* 1968, **21**, 241-267.

Lee, T. Psychology of spatial orientation. *Architectural Association Quarterly,* 1970, **1**, 11-15.

Lösch, A. *Economics of location.* Translated from 2nd edition by W. H. Waglom. New Haven: Yale Univ. Press, 1954.

Marble, D. F., & Bowlby, S. R. Shopping alternatives and recurrent travel patterns. In F. E. Horton (Ed.), Geographic studies of urban transportation and network analysis. *Northwestern Studies in Geography,* Evanston, Illinois: Northwestern Univ. Press, 1968, No. 16.

Nicosia, F. N. *Consumer decision processes: Marketing and advertising implications.* Englewood Cliffs, New Jersey: Prentice-Hall, 1966.

Rogers, D. The role of search and learning in consumer space behavior: The case of urban in-migrants. Unpublished masters thesis, Univ. of Wisconsin, 1970.

Rushton, G. Analysis of spatial behavior by revealed space preferences. *Annals of the Association of American Geographers,* 1969, **59**, 391-400. (a)

Rushton, G. The scaling of locational preferences. In K. R. Cox & R. G. Golledge (Eds.), Behavioral problems in geography: A symposium. *Department of Geography Discussion Paper.* Evanston, Illinois: Northwestern Univ. Press, 1969, No. 17. (b)

Rushton, G. Temporal change in place preference structures. *Proceedings of the Association of American Geographers,* 1969, 129-133. (c)

Saarinen, T. F. Image of the Chicago Loop. Unpublished manuscript, Univ. of Chicago, 1964.

Wilmott, P. Social research and new communities. *Journal of the American Institute of Planners.* 1967, **33**, 387-397.

Zannaras, G. An empirical analysis of urban neighborhood perception. Unpublished masters thesis, Ohio State Univ., 1969.

Chapter IV

Learning from Las Vegas

Colquhoun, A. Typology and design method. *Arena, Architectural Association Journal,* June, 1967.

Hecksher, A. *The public happiness.* New York: Antheneum, 1962.

Le Corbusier. *Towards a new architecture.* Translated by F. Etchells. London Architectural Press, 1927. (Reprinted: 1948.)

Chapter V

Introduction

Lewin, K. Action research and minority problems. *Journal of Social Issues,* 1946, **2,** 34-46.

Proshansky, H. M., Ittelson, W. H., & Rivlin, L. G. (Eds.). *Environmental psychology: Man and his physical setting.* New York: Holt, 1970.

Reading 3: The influence of the physical environment on behavior: Some basic assumptions.

Reading 16: Freedom of choice and behavior in a physical setting.

Reading 43: The environmental psychology of a psychiatric ward.

Reading 65: The use of behavioral maps in environmental psychology.

Environmental Design Implications of a Changing Health Care System

Fellman, G., & Brandt, B. Working-class protest against an urban highway. *Environment and Behavior,* 1971, **3,** 61-79.

Garfield, S. R. The delivery of medical care. *Scientific American,* 1970, **222**(4), 15-23.

Glasscote, R. M., Sanders, D. S., Forstenzer, H. M., & Foley, A. R. *The community mental health center. An analysis of existing models.* Washington, D.C.: The Joint Information Service of the American Psychiatric Association and the National Association for Mental Health, 1964.

Kreidberg, M. B., Field, H. H., Highlands, D., Kennedy, D. A., & Katz, G. *Problems of pediatric hospital design. Study for new design concepts for children's hospitals.* Boston: Boston Floating Hospital, 1965.

Schwartz, W. B. Medicine and the computer: The promise and problems of change. *New England Journal of Medicine,* 1970, **283**, 1257-1264.

Weeks, J. Indeterminate architecture. *Transactions of the Bartlett Society*, 1964, **1**.

Chapter VI

Experimental Studies of Environment Perception

Alexander, C. Major changes in environmental form required by social and psychological form. *Ekistics,* 1969, **28**, 78-85.

Allport, G., & Pettigrew, T. Cultural influence on the perception of movement: The trapezoidal illusion among the Zulus. *Journal of Abnormal and Social Psychology,* 1957, **55**, 104-113.

Antonovsky, H. F., & Ghent, L. Cross-cultural consistency of children's preference for the orientation of figures. *American Journal of Psychology,* 1964, 77, 295-297.

Appleyard, D. Styles and methods of structuring a city. *Environment and Behavior,* 1970, **2**, 100-117.

Appleyard, D., & Lintell, M. *Environmental quality of city streets.* Berkeley: Univ. of California, Institute for Urban and Regional Development, 1970.

Appleyard, D., Lynch, K., & Meyer, J. R. *The view from the road.* Cambridge, Massachusetts: M.I.T. Press, 1964.

Beck, R. Spatial meaning and the properties of the environment. In D. Lowenthal (Ed.), Environmental perception and behavior. *Department of Geography Research Paper.* Chicago: Univ. of Chicago Press, 1967, No. 109.

Birren, F. *Color, form and space.* New York: Rheinhold, 1961.

Blaut, J. M., McCleary, G. F., & Blaut, A. S. Environmental mapping in young children. Unpublished manuscript, Clark Univ., 1970.

Blaut, J. M., & Stea, D. Place learning. *Place Perception Research Reports.* Worcester, Mass.: Clark Univ., 1969, No. 4.

Blaut, J. M., & Stea, D. Studies of geographic learning. Unpublished manuscript, Clark Univ., 1970.

Brower, S. N. Territoriality, the exterior spaces: The signs we learn to read. *Landscape,* autumn, 1965, 9-12.

Burnham, C. A., & Grimm, C. T. Selecting visual properties of architectural surfaces: A psychological approach. Paper presented at the Architects Researchers Conference, Cincinatti, 1970.

Burton, I. Cultural and personality variables in the perception of natural hazards. Unpublished manuscript, Univ. of Toronto, 1970.

Campbell, R. D. Personality as an element of regional geography. *Annals of the Association of American Geographers,* 1968, **58**, 748-759.

Canter, D. Attitudes and perception in architecture. *Architectural Association Quarterly,* 1961, **1**, 24-31.

Canter, D. An intergroup comparison of connotative dimensions in architecture. *Environment and Behavior,* 1969, **1**, 37-48.

Canter, D., & Wools, R. *The subjective assessment of the environment* and *A technique for the subjective appraisal of buildings.* Glasgow: Univ. of Strathclyde, Building Performance Research Unit, 1969.

Carp, F. M. *Environmental experiences and levels of adaptation to changed surroundings.* Palo Alto: American Institutes for Research, 1968.

Carr, S. *The city of the mind.* Paper commissioned for the Conference of the American Institute of Planners, 1966.

Carr, S., & Schissler, D. The city as a trip. *Environment and Behavior,* 1969, **1**, 7-35.

Chermayeff, S., & Alexander, C. *Community and privacy: Toward a new architecture of humanism.* New York: Doubleday, 1963.

Collins, J. B. Some verbal dimensions of architectural space perception. *Architectural Psychology Newsletter,* 1968, **2**, 4-5.

Collins, J. B. Perceptual dimensions of space validated against behavioral criteria. *Man–Environment Systems,* 1970, S 24.

Craik, K. H. The comprehension of the everyday physical environment. *Journal of the American Institute of Planners,* 1968, **34**, 29-37. (a)

Craik, K. H. Human responsiveness to landscape: An environmental psychological perspective. *Student Publications of the School of Design.* Raleigh, North Carolina: North Carolina State Univ., 1968. (b)

Craik, K. H. *Assessing environmental dispositions.* Berkeley: Univ. of California, Institute of Personality Assessment and Research, 1969.

Craik, K. H. Environmental psychology. In K. H. Craik, B. Kleinmuntz, R. L. Rosnow, R. Rosenthal, J. A. Cheyne, & R. H. Walters, *New directions in psychology 4.* New York: Holt, 1970.

DeJonge, D. Images of urban areas. *Journal of the American Institute of Planners,* 1962, **28**, 266-276.

Deregowski, J. B. Difficulties in pictorial depth perception in Africa. *British Journal of Psychology,* 1968, **59**, 195-204.

Downs, R. M. The cognitive structure of an urban shopping center. *Environment and Behavior,* 1970, **2**, 13-39.

Downs, R. M., & Stea, D. (Eds.). *Cognitive mapping: Images of spatial environment.* Chicago: Aldine, 1971.

Ekman, G., & Bratfisch, O. Subjective distance and emotional involvement: A psychological mechanism. *Acta Psychologica,* 1965, **24**, 430-437.

Environmental Research Foundation. Perception of architectural aspects of psychiatric treatment environment. *Architectural Environment and Human Behavior,* 1968.

Epstein, W. *Varieties of perceptual learning.* New York: McGraw-Hill, 1967.

Firey, W. Sentiment and symbolism as ecological variables. *American Sociological Review,* 1945, **10**, 140-148.

Goodman, S. Analysis of blight measurement methods in community renewal programs of eleven cities. Unpublished manuscript, Washington Univ., 1968.

Gulick, J. Images of an Arab city. *Journal of the American Institute of Planners,* 1963, **29**, 179-198.

Halldane, J. F. *Architecture and visual perception.* Berkeley: Univ. of California Press, 1968. (a)

Halldane, J. F. *Psychophysical synthesis of environmental systems.* Berkeley: California Book Co., 1968. (b)

Hallowell, A. I. *Culture and experience.* Philadelphia: Univ. of Pennsylvania, 1957.

Hershberger, R. G. A study of meaning and architecture. *Man and his Environment Newsletter,* 1968, **1**, 6-7.

Hesselgren, S. *The language of architecture.* Lund, Sweden: Studentlitteratur, 1967.

Holmberg, L., Almgren, S., Söderpalm, A. C., & Küller, R. The perception of volume content of rectangular rooms. Comparison between model and full scale experiments. *Psychological Research Bulletin,* 1967, **7** (9).

Holmberg, L., Küller, R., & Tidblom, I. Stability of individual and group data in the perception of volume content of rectangular rooms as measured by production and an estimation method. *Psychological Research Bulletin,* 1966, **6**(7).

Ittelson, W. H. The perception of the large-scale environment. Paper presented to the New York Academy of Science, New York, 1970.

Izumi, K. An analysis for the design of hospital quarters for the neuropsychiatric patient. *Mental Hospitals,* 1957, **8**, 31-32.

Izumi, K. LSD and architectural design. Unpublished manuscript, Univ. of Saskatchewan Regina Campus, 1967.

Kasmar, J. The development of a semantic scale for the description of the physical environment. Unpublished doctoral dissertation, Louisiana State Univ., 1965.

Kasmar, J. The development of a usable lexicon of environmental descriptors. *Environment and Behavior*, 1970, **2**, 153-169.

Kasmar, J., Griffin, W. V., & Mauritzen, J. H. Effect of environmental surroundings on outpatients' mood and perception of psychiatrists. *Journal of Consulting and Clinical Psychology*, 1968, **32**, 223-226.

Kates, R. W. Hazard and choice perception in flood plain management. *Department of Geography Research Paper.* Chicago: Univ. of Chicago Press, 1962, No. 78.

Kates, R. W. Stimulus and symbol: The view from the bridge. *Journal of Social Issues,* 1966, **22**, 21-28.

Kates, R. W., & Wohlwill, J. (Eds.). Man's response to the physical environment. *Journal of Social Issues,* 1966, **22**(4), 1-141.

Ladd, F. C. Black youths view their environment. *Environment and Behavior,* 1970, **2**, 74-99.

Lansing, J. B., & Marans, R. W. Evaluation of neighborhoods. *Journal of the American Institute of Planners,* 1969, **35**, 195-199.

Lee, T. Perceived distance as a function of direction in the city. *Environment and Behavior*, 1970, **2**, 40-51.

Little, A. D., Inc. *Response to the roadside environment.* The Outdoor Advertising Association of America, 1968.

Lowenthal, D. America as scenery. *Geographical Review,* 1966, **56**, 115-118.

Lowenthal, D. (Ed.). *An analysis of environmental perception* (2nd ed.) Interim Report to Resources for the Future, Inc., 1967. (a)

Lowenthal, D. (Ed.). Environmental perception and behavior. *Department of Geography Research Paper,* Chicago: Univ. of Chicago, 1967, No. 109. (b)

Lowenthal, D. Geography, experience and imagination: Towards a geographical epistemology. In F. Dohrs & L. Sommers (Eds.), *Cultural geography: Selected readings.* New York: Crowell-Collier, 1967. (c)

Lowenthal, D. Environmental perception project: Relevance of research hypotheses for environmental design. *Man and his Environment Newsletter,* 1968, **1**, 3-6. (a)

Lowenthal, D. The American scene. *Geographical Review,* 1968, **58**, 61-88. (b)

Lowenthal, D. *Environmental and semantic responses: Comparative studies in environmental perception.* New York: American Geographical Society, 1971.

Lynch, K. The form of cities. *Scientific American,* 1954, **190**(4), 55-63.

Lynch, K. *The image of the city.* Cambridge, Massachusetts: M.I.T. & Harvard Univ. Press, 1960.

Lynch, K. *Site planning.* Cambridge, Massachusetts: M.I.T. Press, 1962.

Lynch, K. The city as environment. In *Scientific American* (Ed.), *Cities.* New York: Knopf, 1965.

Lynch, K., & Rivkin, M. A walk around the block. *Landscape,* spring, 1959, 24-34.

Maslow, A. H., & Mintz, N. L. Effects of esthetic surroundings: II. Prolonged and repeated experience in a 'beautiful' and an 'ugly' room. *Journal of Psychology,* 1956, **41**, 459.

Michelson, W. An empirical analysis of urban environmental preferences. *Journal of the American Institute of Planners,* 1966, **32**, 355-360.
Michelson, W. Urban sociology as an aid to urban development, some research strategies. *Journal of the American Institute of Planners,* 1968. (a)
Michelson, W. Social insights to guide the design of housing for low income families. *Ekistics,* 1968, **25**, 252-255. (b)
Milgram, S. The experience of living in cities. *Science,* 1970, **167**, 1461-1468.
Nahemow, L. Research in a novel environment. *Environment and Behavior,* 1971, **3**, 81-102.
Newman, O. Physical parameters of defensible space. Unpublished manuscript, New York Univ., 1969.
Osmond, H. Function as the basis of psychiatric ward design. *Mental Hospitals,* 1957, **8**, 23-30.
Osmond, H. The relationship between architect and psychiatrist. *Psychiatric Architecture,* 1961, 16-20.
Osmond, H. Design must meet patient's human needs. *Modern Hospital,* 1966.
Parr, A. E. Mind and milieu. *Sociological Inquiry,* 1963, **33**, 19-24.
Passonneau, J. R. The emergence of city form. In W. Z. Hirsch (Ed.), *Urban life and form.* New York: Holt, 1965.
Payne, I. Pupillary responses to architectural stimuli. *Man–Environment Systems,* 1969, S 11.
Peterson, G. L., Bishop, R. L., & Fitzgerald, R. W. The quality of visual residential environments: Perceptions and preferences. *Man–Environment Systems,* 1969, S 13.
Rappaport, A., & Hawkes, R. The perception of urban complexity. *Journal of the American Institute of Planners,* 1970, **36**, 106-111.
Rasmussen, S. *Experiencing architecture.* New York: M.I.T. Press & Wiley, 1959.
Rock, I. *The nature of perceptual adaptation.* New York: Basic Books, 1966.
Saarinen, T. F. Perception of drought hazard on the Great Plains. *Department of Geography Research Paper.* Chicago: Univ. of Chicago, 1966, No. 106.
Saarinen, T. F. Perception of environment. *Commission on College Geography Resource Paper.* Washington, D.C.: Association of American Geographers, 1969, No. 5.
Sanoff, H. Visual attributes of the physical environment. Paper prepared for the American Psychological Association Conference, San Francisco, August 1968.
Segall, M. H., Campbell, D. T., & Herskovits, M. J. Some psychological theory and predictions on cultural differences. *Influence of culture on visual perception.* Indianapolis: Bobbs-Merrill, 1966.
Sewell, W. R. D. Environmental perceptions and attitudes of engineers and public health officials. Paper presented at American Psychological Association convention, Miami Beach, 1970. Also in *Environment and Behavior,* 1971, **3**, 23-60.
Shafer, E. L., Jr. Perception of natural environments. *Environment and Behavior,* 1969, **1**, 71-82.
Sonnenfeld, J. Environmental perception and adaptation level in the Arctic. In D. Lowenthal (Ed.), Environmental perception and behavior. *Department of Geography Research Paper.* Chicago: Univ. of Chicago, 1967, No. 109.
Sonnenfeld, J. Equivalence and distortion of the perceptual environment. *Environment and Behavior,* 1969, **1**, 83-99.
Southworth, M. The sonic environment of cities. *Environment and Behavior,* 1969, **1**, 49-70.

Spivak, M. Sensory distortion in tunnels and corridors. *Hospital and Community Psychiatry*, 1967, **18**, 12-18.

Sprout, H., & Sprout, M. *The ecological perspective on human affairs.* Princeton, New Jersey: Princeton Univ. Press, 1965.

Stea, D. Environmental perception and cognition: Toward a model for "mental maps". *Student Publications of the School of Design.* Raleigh, North Carolina: North Carolina State Univ., 1969. (a)

Stea, D. The measurement of mental maps: An experimental model for measuring conceptual spaces. In K. R. Cox & R. G. Golledge (Eds.), Behavioral problems in geography: A symposium. *Department of Geography Discussion Paper.* Evanston, Illinois: Northwestern Univ. Press, 1969, No. 17. (b)

Stea, D. Bibliography of mental mapping studies and related topics. Unpublished manuscript.

Stea, D., & Blaut, J. M. Notes toward a developmental theory of spatial learning. In J. Arches & C. Eastman (Eds.), *EDRA two. Proceedings of the second annual Environmental Design Research Association conference.* Pittsburgh, Pennsylvania: Carnegie Press, 1970.

Stea, D., & Downs, R. M. From the outside looking in at the inside looking out. *Environment and Behavior,* 1970, **2**, 3-12.

Steinitz, C. Meaning and the congruence of urban form and activity. *Journal of the American Insitute of Planners,* 1968, **34**, 233-248.

Strauss, A. L. (Ed.). *The American city, a sourcebook of urban imagery.* Chicago: Aldine, 1968.

Swinburne, H. H. The environment we see. In W. R. Ewald (Ed.), *Environments for man: The next fifty years.* Bloomington: Indiana Univ. Press, 1967.

Van der Ryn, S., & Boie, W. R. *Value measurement and visual factors in the urban environment.* Berkeley: Univ. of California, College of Environmental Design, 1963.

Vigier, F. C. An experimental approach to urban design. *Journal of the American Institute of Planners,* 1965, **31**, 21-31.

Wastlund, H., & Wihervuori, K. Stockholm i vart inre. *Att bo.* Translated by Swedish Consulate, New Orleans, La. Stockholm, 1962, 183-194.

Webber, M. M., & Webber, C. C. Culture, territoriality and the elastic mile. Vol. 1. In H. W. Eldvedge (Ed.), *Taming megalopolis.* Garden City, New York: Doubleday, 1967.

Weiss, R. S., & Boutourline, S., Jr. *Fairs, exhibits, pavilions, and the audiences.* Author, 1962.

Winkel, G. H., Malek, R., & Thiel, P. Individual differences in response to the roadside environment. *Environment and Behavior,* 1969, **1**, 199-223.

Wohlwill, J. F. The physical environment: A problem for the psychology of stimulation. *Journal of Social Issues,* 1966, **22**, 29-38.

Author Index

Numbers in italics refer to the pages on which the complete references are listed.

Subject Index

H

J

K

L

M

N

P